A Brief Miscellaneous Narrative
of the More Early Part of the Life of L. Tilmon,
Pastor of a Colored Methodist Congregational Church in the City of New York:
By
Levin Tilmon
[1807-1863]

CONTENTS

A BRIEF MISCELLANEOUS NARRATIVE
OF THE
MORE EARLY PART OF THE LIFE OF
L. TILMON,
PASTOR OF A COLORED METHODIST CONGREGATIONAL CHURCH IN THE CITY OF NEW YORK.

WRITTEN BY HIMSELF.

JERSEY CITY:
W. W. & L. A. PRATT, PRINTERS, SENTINEL BUILDINGS.
1853.

LARGE PRINT EDITION

PREPARED FOR PUBLICATION

BY

HISTORIC PULISHING

ISBN-10: 1946640336

PREFACE.

The brief narrative I have introduced to the public, has been hastily thrown together. In view of some of the events of the more earlier part of my life, the thoughts of which has always given me a detested hatred to the system of American Slavery. Having thus formed an early impression from what I have suffered, that Slavery was wrong, against which I have felt it to be an imperative duty, to make an expression of my feelings. This I have attempted several times, but have become discouraged, for the want of a liberal education, but of which I have been robbed by the evil genius of American Slavery. In reviewing my past life, I feel that I have been the child of misfortune, being deprived of all early advantages. I have been thrown upon my own resources, upon which I have had to depend. Having quite a zest for learning, and to acquire information, I have been driven to burn the midnight lamp, until my health has become much impaired. For this and the neglect of my youthful training, I lay to the charge of the American people; whose soil of the sunny South my father and mother had to till and cultivate. This has not been their condition alone, but it has been, and still is, the condition of more than three millions of Africa's sons and daughters, that now live upon the soil of the American continent. There are two positions which the colored people occupy in this country: First, as slaves, and Second, as nominal freemen. We ask, what is the condition of the slaves in a land of whips and chains? The apologist for slavery says, "that they are better off than the latter." We admit that the condition of the latter is bad enough; but not to be equalled with the suffering of the slaves, for they are subjected to a condition below that of the brute: denied of all that man holds dear to himself upon earth. They dare not say that their souls are their own, or speak in their own defence. Poor, helpless people! Their manhood is crushed--their rights are trampled in the dust--the female virtue is disregarded--mothers and fathers have their children torn away from their embraces--wives and husbands are separated--brothers and sisters are parted, and yet the apologist for slavery says, "that the slaves are better off than the free blacks of the north." This is not true, for the slave is in every way deprived of his God-given rights, which are life, liberty, and the pursuit of happiness.

While the nominally free colored man of the north has the right to speak, think, and act for himself, in this respect his situation is widely different, yet he is denied the right of suffrage in common with his white fellow citizens. It is a fact that cannot be denied, that the children, to a greater or lesser extent, inherit the principles of their parents. We offer this as an argument in the defence of the colored people of the north, for they are the descendants of slave parents, to a greater or lesser extent, and their condition would be vastly different if the right of suffrage was to them extended. The Hon. Henry Clay, the genius and pride of the American people, said in a late speech, that the condition of the blacks of the north was infinitely worse than that of the slaves in the south. He says when visiting the north, the blacks are excluded from the workshops, and the free blacks content themselves in performing menial labor, such as coachmen, waiters, cartmen, etc. This is true, and why is it that they are excluded from the northern mechanical workshops? I answer, because of American prejudices. Hence, the colored freeman is compelled to take up with such employments as are thrown in his way. And when we look for him, where do we find him? Upon the gallant ship, amid the humming cords, or behind the striped pole, and yet there is scarcely a depot in America upon which the sun shines, but what receives the products of the toil of the poor American slave. We also see it in the delicate rice dish, and in the flowing bowl, and no less so in the glowing silks that adorn the delicate American females. In view of the above, the enjoyments and independence of the American people on the one hand, and the condition of the colored people upon the other hand, then let us ask, where is the colored man that has a tongue, and dare not speak out the sentiments of his soul? and where is hand that can use the pen, and refuses to do it? Let every colored man adopt the sentiment of the noble patriot Patrick Henry, "Give me liberty or give me death."

This narrative is written by one whose body and mind have felt the blighting and withering effects of Slavery, and who is anxious to do what he can for the liberation of those of his race, who are still suffering in bondage.

It may be asked, why do you attempt to write upon a subject upon which such floods of light are already poured? I answer--because I wish to express indelibly, my opposition and hatred to Slavery, and to reveal some facts which have not yet been presented to the public--and to reveal them in such a manner, that they may speak when I am dead.

Facts lie at the foundation of all true reasoning, and the author contents himself with being able to present the foundation from which others may reason.

The reader will not look for finished style, nor for strictly correct sentences, from one whose time for mental improvement was spent in Slavery.

The author thinks the above a sufficient apology for presenting his humble effort to the public, and hopes that it may, in some measure, subserve the cause of freedom.

NARRATIVE.

CHAPTER I.

I was born in the State of Maryland, Carolina Co., in the year 1807. As near as I can recollect, my father and mother were both slaves. They had eight children, three boys and five girls, who were all slaves. My mother and her four younger children were manumitted and set free when we were quite small, (myself and three younger sisters.) My two elder brothers and sisters were still held in bondage. My brother Charles died in the year 1827. Though a slave, thank God, he died a Freeman in Christ Jesus. In his dying moments he called his mistress to his bed-side, and told her that he was going to Heaven. He then bid the world adieu, and expired with a fall assurance of a blessed immortality. My father, elder brother, and two sisters, were left behind to endure the ills of a cruel bondage. My two sisters, in connection with all other female slaves in the South, were deprived of the protection of their virtue, which is disregarded and trampled in the dust, by the amorous aspirant, who delights in seducing the character of the helpless female. The elder of my two sisters became a mother by the son of her own master. This as a matter of course created a very unpleasant state of feeling in her master's family, for which plans were soon devised for her removal to the far South. Accordingly, she was sent some distance from the house one evening, to milk, as is usually done in the South; and while in the act of milking, several ruffians who were concealed in the standing corn, jumped over the fence, seized, gagged, and dragged her away, disregarding her shrieks or cries.

The next was my sister Violette, who was the favorite of my youth. My affections were more strongly drawn towards her than any one of the others of my brothers or sisters. A month had scarcely passed away before another nefarious scheme was plotted for the purpose of reducing her to a more cruel state of chattled slavery. I have never seen nor heard of either of them since. This was in the year 1823, as I have been informed since.

> God moves in a mysterious way,
> His wonders to perform;
> He plants his footsteps in the sea,
> And rides upon the storm.

> His purposes will ripen fast,
> Unfolding ev'ry hour;
> The bud may have a bitter taste,
> But sweet will be the flower.

Shortly after this the judgments of God were brought to bear upon that man and his family. His farm of five hundred acres of land, and all that he had, were swept away, and that cruel son, who had caused a slave mother's heart to bleed, died a miserable death, and his father was driven by famine with his saddle bags to beg his bread from door to door, and at last died a vagrant. I now have a father and one brother, if living, who are still held in bondage.

CHAPTER II.

At the age of eight years, my mother bound me out to learn the farming business, with a man by the name of D. D--n, who was the son of a Hicksite Quaker preacher. He married in a Quaker family, and settled in the upper part of the State of Delaware, near the place called Isborn and James' Limestone Quarries. I was to have six month's schooling, and at the age of twenty-one, two suits of clothing. With this understanding between him and my mother, I was removed from the state of Maryland to his place of residence, in the State of Delaware. After I had been there some time, (as is usual for a child,) the thoughts of my mother, my little brothers and sisters, my native land, and childhood scenes, rushed upon my mind. O! I shall never forget that day, when I stood as I thought with my face towards the land of my birth, my bosom heaved with sighs of sorrow, my heart throbbed with violent emotions, and the scalding tears coursed down my cheeks. My cry was, O! my mother! my mother!

My employment was to take care of the children, and to perform such other duties as I was capable of performing. As soon as I was large enough I was put to the team and on the farm.

And now a new era in the history of my life commenced. I was half fed, half clothed, and worked late and early. And now I began to realize the bitterness and the cruel workings of American slavery, in a land of strangers, with no kind mother to care for my wants, or to relieve my woes. His wife was of the Quaker origin, she was a very kind and tender hearted woman; but he was a demon in human shape. There were three servants in the family, myself, and another colored boy by the name of Irvin Steel, and a white girl by the name of Sally Agin, who on many occasions shared in sufferings with us. I remember on one occasion, she got her feet badly frosted, so much so, that she was unable to attend to her usual employment. Poor girl! While in this state of suffering, he took umbrage at her for some trivial cause or other, and beat her unmercifully, from which, she never recovered, but died shortly afterward. Soon after this, his wife died also, leaving behind two children, a boy and girl. Poor woman! she died heart-broken on account of his cruel treatment; for he was cruel, both to man and brute. Now a sad change took place in the affairs. The farm was rented out. My fellow-servant's time, was sold to a man by the name of John Irvin, who lived on a place near Stanton, in the State of Delaware, called Bread and Cheese Island; he was said to be a very kind man. I remained on the farm, (with the man who rented it,) for the term of one year. At the expiration of which, it was rented to another man by the name of John Wiser, who was a noted character, for horse racing and trading. He drank very freely, and was away a great deal from home, spending his time at taverns. He also, was a very cruel man; and used to beat me shamefully, when he would indulge in his drunken sprees! He used to make me desecrate the sabbath by grazing the horses in the locks of the fences. I remember on one sabbath, he came home, and sent me to the stable with the horse, and while I was there, he came, and for no cause whatever, he seized a large white oak club, and commenced beating me unmercifully, and I believe would have killed me, had I have not got out of his reach. He used to call himself a great bully, and was very annoying to his neighbors. I remember one day, he went to Wilmington, Delaware, and while there he became very much intoxicated, and on his return home, he fell in company with a man against whom he had an old grudge; an altercation ensued between them, in which he was severely beaten, which curbed his quarrelsome disposition, for some time after.

CHAPTER III.

At the expiration of the year the farm underwent another change, and I was put to live with a man by the name of James Covington, who lived a mile and a half distance from my former place of residence. He and his wife were of poor origin, and lived very disagreeably together. This as a matter of course, increased my sufferings, for both of them were very unkind to me, and he was a man that drank very freely. He used to follow the lime-burning business; and one day while at the lime-kiln, a colored man was passing by, when he accosted him, and soon discovered that he was a fugitive. He now set to work to devise a plan for his detection. He (the said Covington) said he wanted to hire a man, and immediately entered into arrangements, for so much, per month, to husk corn. I was absent, at the quarries with the team, for a load of stone, and was not aware of what was going on. Poor fellow, it was but a trap set to ensnare him. Upon my returning home in the evening, to my surprise, I saw a colored man in the lot husking corn. I had no opportunity of learning from him the facts of the case, but on my going to bed in the evening, the wife of said Covington told me not to sleep in the same room with that man, for they intended to take him away that night. This alarmed me very much. Accordingly, early in the morning, the said Covington, with a band of ruffians, all mounted upon horses, took the poor fellow in confinement, and started off for the purpose of conveying him back to his owners. I learned afterwards, upon their arrival, that his master seized a large bludgeon and split his skull open, and then placed him in the smoke house in confinement.

During my stay in that wretched family, my miseries and sufferings were augmented. Mrs. Covington sent me one day to the spring for water; and upon my return, for some trivial cause unknown to me, she seized the butt end of an old whip stock, and struck me over the head, which caused the blood to flow profusely. At this moment I threw off all restraint, and a serious altercation ensued. I then made up my mind to remain no longer, but to return home to my old master.

On my arrival at his place, my old master was absent; and upon his return in the evening, I related to him, what had occurred between Mrs. Covington and myself; and told him that I could not live with such people; but he made little or no reply, and that was just what I expected. This was on a Saturday night, and the next morning, to my surprise, who should I discover coming across the field, but Covington. He came up, and he and my old master had some private conversation together. He then said to me, come, you must go home with me! and I refused to go; he then laid hold of me, and we had quite a struggle; however, he succeeded in getting the better of me, and I was compelled to submit.

Shortly after, my old master married, and I was taken back again on the farm. He married in a very respectable family by the name of H. M., (formerly residents of Bucks Co., Pa.) who are residents of the State of Delaware, and were members of the Church of England. His wife was a very fine woman, but his treatment towards her was similar to that of his first wife's. About this time he was expelled from the Society of Friends, on account of bad conduct. I was now between the age of 16 and 17 years, and had determined to run away, as I did not feel willing to endure the cruelties and hardships of a chattled slavery any longer. But no favorable opportunity had, as yet, presented itself; and one day, while at work in the lime stone quarries, he took umbrage at one of the team horses, (for he was a very passionate and hasty man,) he seized a bludgeon about seven feet long, and knocked the shaft horse in the head. This was on a Thursday afternoon, and about the same hour on the following Thursday he was at work near the same spot, when the whole bank caved in upon him, and broke his leg. He was then conveyed home, and the Doctor sent for. I now thought that this was my time to escape. Accordingly, on the following Saturday morning I got up quite early, gathered my clothes together, and tied them up in a bundle, and started off in search of a land of freedom. Just as I left the yard, going towards the woods, his wife's sister came out at the garden door. I kept my bundle concealed, in front of me, thinking that she would suppose that I was gone for oven wood; as that was my usual employment on Saturday morning. But not returning within the usual time, they supposed that all was not right, and immediately went in pursuit of my clothes, and not finding them, they concluded that I had ran away.

CHAPTER IV.

I arrived at Wilmington, Delaware, about eleven o'clock, a distance of some ten miles on my journey. In passing up the street towards the main street that led out to Brandywine, I spied the man that lived next neighbor to my old boss. He was there for the purpose of attending market: however he did not happen to see me; and I soon turned the corner and took another street, and went on. Just as I got to the bridge, leading over the Brandwine creek, I met a colored woman, and enquired of her, if that was the straight road to Philadelphia, and she asked me if I was going there, when I told her I was. She then asked me if I was not a runaway. I said no, I had a mother there and I was going to see her. She then told me that I had better not go on foot, that if I did, I would be taken up; and that I had better go by water, and that there was a man, by the name of Capt. Jackes, that was going to sail for Philadelphia that afternoon; and that he would take me, for he was a very fine man. I took her to be a friend; and with the advice she had given me, I started off in search of Capt. Jackes, and his vessel. I went into a mill to enquire, where there were two men loading a vessel. I asked them if that was Capt. Jackes' vessel; they stopped and looked at me. I soon began to think that I was in the wrong pew; and one of them asked me where I was from, and I told him I was from the country. He asked me where I was going. I told him I was going to Philadelphia, to see my mother. He then wanted to know with whom I had lived. I told him that I had lived with a man by the name of Dorsey, in the suburbs of Wilmington. He said that I was a runaway; I told him I was not.

He then said that he would see about it; and then commenced putting on his shoes, and told me to stay until he should return. I soon began to think that this state of things would not do for me, and as soon as he was gone, whipped out from the mill, and ran down the bank, and seeing a vessel which I supposed was Capt. Jackes', I made an attempt to jump on board, but losing my balance, I fell into the creek, and came near being drowned. I scrambled and succeeded in getting hold of the rigging of a vessel, and thus I saved myself from a watery grave. Reader, you may judge, what must have been my present state of feelings. Before me was the boon of Freedom, and behind me was the demon of American Slavery braying upon my track. I hastened into another mill, and inquired of a gentleman, for Capt. Jackes. He pointed him out to me, whom I approached, and asked him if he was going to Philadelphia that afternoon? He said he was. I told him I had a mother there, whom I wanted to see, and asked him, would he take me; he said he would. I then went over the creek with him to his place of residence, and spent the afternoon. In the evening I went aboard of the vessel, and went to bed, being weary and fatigued, soon fell asleep, and knew nothing more until the morning, when I found myself upon the broad waters of the Delaware. This was a source of gratification and astonishment to me. I now felt that I was beyond the reach of my pursuers. I was highly delighted in viewing the scenes, such as I had never seen before. The gallant vessel moved onward to her place of destination, bearing upon her decks a panting fugitive, sighing for liberty.

Just as the sun was setting, we hove in sight of the city of Philadelphia, but were detained several hours, (owing to a calm.) I retired to bed, and in the morning came on deck, and found the vessel lying alongside the dock. I stood gazing, my mind being filled with wonder and astonishment. Partly bewildered at beholding the strange scenes, and listening to the buz of a crowded city. The drays were dashing along the wharves, and the masts of the gallant ships, to me, looked like a forest. However, I soon felt a peculiar anxiety to go ashore, to satisfy my mind in observing the curiosities of a large metropolis. Thus amusing myself for the day, I returned in the evening to the vessel again. The following morning I again went ashore, in pursuit of employment, and fell in company with several boys, with whom I spent the forenoon, until it was finally agreed that we should go in search of something to eat. I asked the boy who made the proposal, "Where are you going to get it?" The reply was, "Never mind, come and go with me." In going up into the city, we went into an alley called Black Horse Alley. The said boy went up to a door and rang the bell, when a lady answered the call. The boy pulled off his hat, made a polite bow, and assuming a most pitiful face, said, "Please ma'am, give me some cold victuals?" She went away, and soon returned with a dish full; all of which he received in his hat, to share among his comrades. And I in turning from the door, in casting my eye upward, I spied a sign, with a horse upon it; the thought at once occurred to me, that perhaps I might get employment there. And upon my arrival at the door, I saw a gentleman whom I asked if he wanted to hire a boy? He said that he did not, but asked me if I was not a runaway. I told him no, but that I had a mother here somewhere, and I wanted a situation, until such time that I could find her. He then asked me where I was from, when I told him that I was from the country; and as I turned away from the door, he called his mother and said, here is a boy, do you want to hire one? She answered 'no,' and on coming to the door, asked me what my name was? I told her it was Joseph Hutchinson. "And what can you do?" asked the lady. I told her that I could take care of horses, act as waiter, &c. "What wages do you ask?" I answered two dollars per month, when she said, "I guess I'll take you." At this moment my heart leaped for joy, with the prospects of a home, and of making money.

CHAPTER V.

I entered upon the duties of my new home with renewed vigor and cheerfulness, and was very active for the purpose of making money. One day while there, a gentleman gave me a twenty-five cent piece, and I thought that I was rich, but it did not seem bulky enough for me, so I went to the hostler, and asked him to change it for me, for which he gave twenty-five coppers. O! I thought that I was now rich, to be sure; and that I must now have something to carry my money in, so away I went and bought me a Buckskin money purse. By this time, the family had become quite attached to me; and took quite an interest in my welfare. The week rolled away pleasantly, and the Sabbath came on. The landlady told me to sweep up the yard &c.; and while I was sweeping, the bells began to ring. I dropped the broom, and away I went, to see if I could see them, and after spending some time in looking upon the church-going crowd, I returned again to my employment without seeing them.

Never shall I forget that morning. It will be a period in the history of my life. I had returned but a short time, when I was called by the landlady to do an errand at the shop, to procure two eggs to make a pudding for dinner. On doing my errand, just as I stepped out of the shop door I spied the gang of boys, whose company I had abandoned a few days previous. I hailed them, for the purpose of relating my success &c. as boys usually do.

Just at that moment I heard a voice calling me by my right name. This startled me. I turned around suddenly and who should I see on the opposite side of the street, but a man by the name of Joshua Wiser, a brother to the man that had lived upon my old master's farm. He was a carpenter by trade, and was then a resident of the city of Philadelphia. He was sitting at the window of a tavern, called Bulls' head. He got up and came to the door, and called me to him. I went, and upon my entering the bar-room, all eyes were upon me; he asked me what I was doing there, and what caused me to run away. I told him that I was not a run-away, and neither was my name Lev., as they used to call me in the country. Neither had I any master. I felt a disposition to conceal the truth under all existing circumstances! He told me I need not deny the truth, for he knew me; just at that moment I heard the landlord say "we had better secure him." And at that suggestion, I gave a hawk, as though I wanted to spit, and stepped towards the door. I made one leap, and a dead foot race ensued, with eggs in hand. I made down towards Chestnut street intending to make for my home. His, (Wiser's) hat fell off; he not stopping to pick it up, pursued close after me, and the cry was "stop thief; stop thief." Having missed my longitude, I partly halted to bethink my way, and as I wheeled, I shot him in the face with one of the eggs. By this time I was surrounded by a crowd, and I looked to see if there was any one who had come to my rescue. I saw none but a few helpless colored females, and their forces were too weak. I was taken back to the tavern, and placed in a room above stairs. At this crisis, my feelings of agony were intense. I thought my heart would break. They offered me brandy to assuage my grief. They next offered me some dinner; truly it was a delicious dish, which I was not in the habit of seeing, much less eating. It was cold slaugh, roast beef, and sweet potatoes. My appetite had left me, and my mind was fraught with grief.

About two o'clock, the said Wiser, in company with another very large man, entered my room, each of them about six feet high. My agony increased. Not yet understanding where my destiny would be, though my thoughts were, that it would be nothing short of Georgia. He told me that I must now come, and go with them. I immediately went down stairs, and upon reaching the door, I saw a horse and gig in readiness for me. I was seated, one upon each side of me, (with pistols in hand,) and we started off, I not knowing where they were going to carry me. However as they proceeded out of the city, I looked ahead and saw a woods, and thought when I got there, I would make another attempt for my freedom; but to my surprise before they got there, they drove up to a large building, and alighted. The big iron bolts and locks, were thrown back for my reception, and I was conducted to a cell, and the iron locks and bolts were turned upon me. In the center of the floor of my cell, was a large iron ring bolt, and one small window, grated with iron bars, in which lay an old copy of the New Testament. In one comer lay one or two old woolen blankets out of which

Imade a bed, and laid myself down to sleep. I was awakened by a knocking at the door of my cell; and I arose and saw a gentleman standing in front of the iron gate. He called to me and asked, "What I was doing there?" I was now willing for the first time to confess the truth. I told him I was there for the cause of running away. After interrogating me, he left. In this situation, I remained for nearly a week. My allowance, once in twenty-four hours, was a half -pound of rye bread, and a quart of cold water. With this treatment I was taken sick, and the family physician was sent to visit me in my cell; during which time many of the prisoners were released.

At times when I would hear the roll called for dismission, O! how I would wish that it was my case: however on the following Friday I was called for; for a moment joy and gladness sprung up, and the next moment my mind was changed to sadness, not knowing what the result would be: however, upon leaving my cell, I spied a crowd of gentlemen in the hall, one of whom was the man (by the name of John Shipley,) who lived on the farm with my old boss. He asked me if I would go home with him without putting him to any trouble, as he had been sent for me, to which I readily replied, I would. I was then taken before a magistrate, where I had a summary hearing; he had brought my indentures with him which the magistrate examined, and pronounced incorrect, but said nevertheless I would have to go home. If I had had then a counsellor my case would have been righted. We then started off, to return to the land of whips and chains, where we arrived about seven o'clock in the evening. Upon my arrival, I was sent for to make my appearance in the room of my old master who was still confined to his bed; when I approached him. "He said, "well sir, you have got back have you?" I told him I had. " What did you runaway for sir?" because I wanted to be free. "Well sir, I will attend to you when I get up." I thought to myself if you do you will have to be smarter than I am. The time seemed to roll away for a few days pleasantly; as I felt that I was now my own master, for the time being; but this state of things did not last long, before the clouds of darkness again covered my horizon. For as soon as he was able to hobble about upon his crutches, and ride upon horseback, he had determined to put me into his pocket. He went from home one day, (I being ignorant of his intention) to an old colored woman called Elcy Williams, who lived at a place called "Hare's Corner," near Christina, Delaware. This old woman lived upon the road side and sold beer and cakes. He had made arrangements with her, as I was subsequently informed, and had sold me to a man in the city of Baltimore, Md., by the name of Woodfork, a notorious Negro-trader. I was sent to the said Elcy Williams, whose house was to be the trap for me. During the day, she was to secrete me in the woods, and at night I was to be concealed in the house until such time as he should come and take me away. The object of my being secreted, was to prevent my being seen by the adjoining neighbors, who should perchance pass by that way to Court. About this time, he had become very much reduced in circumstances; his farm, and all that he owned was in a few days to pass out of his possession, by a public vendue. The law of the State of Delaware, was at that time, that all colored people, whether slaves or apprentices, fared alike; apprentices at the age of 16 or 17, becoming dissatisfied with one master, had a right to choose another. In a day or two after, he had plotted his nefarious scheme for my destruction--he sent me to the mill, and also to do an errand at a place called Stanton, where his first wife's relatives resided, and to see his two children who were then living with an aunt of theirs, by the name of Molly Pierce; she was an excellent woman, it was from her I learnt of what was going on.

> Judge not the Lord by feeble sense,
> But trust him for his grace;
> Behind a frowning providence
> He hides a smiling face.

Mrs. Pierce being fully apprised of the danger to which I was exposed, persuaded me not to return home, but to hasten my escape. I told her no, that the animal I had was blind and could not find its way back. Upon my return home I went to the stable, and while there, the moon shone with magnificent splendor; I looked and saw him on his crutch.es, advancing towards me; and when he approached me, he commenced detailing what he wanted me to do, not being aware that I had on that afternoon learned the whole secret. He commenced by saying,

"Thee knows that to-morrow is my vendue, and thy time will be sold?--thee knows that James Covington and James Holingsworth, both wants thee, and I have determined that they shall not have thee, because they will not treat thee well: but there is a man in Baltimore that wants thee for a waiter? (at that suggestion my mind began to waver; the idea of living in a city, was very desirable to me,) and I want thee to get up to morrow morning early, and go down to Elcy Williams; thee knows where she lives; and she will take thee. I don't want thee to stay about the house in the daytime, but stay in the woods, and in the evening thee can come up to the house, because if thee stays about in the daytime, some of the neighbors will see thee; for they will be passing that way to court; and I will come down to night or to-morrow night upon old Lock, and slip thee off." Upon this understanding, I went to the house and went to bed, not letting him know but what I would do as he had requested. But I did not awake in the morning, until he called me; the sun was now up, and it was too late for me to go to Elcy Williams, for I should have been discovered by the neighbors, and he said, "now if thee will go down here to Jinny Grub's huckleberry swamp, and lay there till evening, and then get up, and go on, for it is very pleasant moonlight nights, and if thee will do as I tell thee, I will give thee my gold watch, and the price of thy freedom clothes." Upon this he started up stairs to get his watch, but soon returned, saying that he could not find it; but that he would look it up and bring it with him. I started off, and went on till I passed by the swamp, and arrived to a high hill, called Quaker Hill; here the roads forked. I stopped with my arms folded, to determine which of these roads to take. The road to the right, would have placed me in hopeless bondage, while the road to the left beyond the reach of the dark demon of American Slavery--beyond the land of whips and chains and blood-thirsty slave holders. I finally determined to pursue the road to the left. In passing by the house where said Wiser lived, (he being from home,) his wife who was standing on the piazza, hailed and told me to hasten my escape.

This gave me to believe that she was fully apprised of the circumstances surrounding my case, and upon my arrival at Stanton, where I had been the previous evening, I called upon Mrs. Pierce, and she told me that I had better hasten on, (with a letter of introduction, she had procured from Squire Craig,) to Judge Richardson who lived upon Quaker Hill, back of Wilmington, Del., where I arrived about twelve o'clock. The Judge was not at home, and I presented the letter to his lady, and upon his return the letter was presented to him, which he read, and wrote me another letter of introduction, to several other gentlemen in Wilmington, by the names of Ziby Ferris, Joseph Bringas, Joseph Grubbs, and others. They were all members of the Society of Friends, and were thorough abolitionists. The information was soon communicated from one to the other, and in the evening they held a meeting of consultation, at the shop of Mr. Ferris, where I was called upon to narrate the whole circumstance; after which, they told me I was not to leave the city, until they had taken action upon my case. They then sent for my own master to meet them in Stanton, and to appear before Squire Craig, which he refused to do.

They made another appointment, and sent an officer for him summoning him to appear before the civil authorities. He made his appearance, and was then compelled to relinquish all further claims to my services. The above named gentlemen interfered in my behalf and restored to me my rights according to the laws of the State of Delaware. It was then agreed upon that I should have the right of choosing a master for myself, with whom I was to serve the remainder of my term, which was four years.

I next went to live with a man by the name of Mr. H. Mitchell, in whose family my old master had married his second wife. Mrs. Mitchell was a very fine, kind-hearted woman. They fed and clothed well, and were very strict and precise in their manners, but very striving and industrious in their habits. To them I am indebted for my religious training: for it was while there, that I felt the first impressions of the need of a Saviour. It was also while with this family, that I received six months schooling.

This is the only advantage that I have ever had of an early education. About this time I had a great zest for learning. On the afternoon of the last day of my going to school, while gathering up my books, the Teacher manifested a degree of sorrow, and said that he was very loth to part with me, (I being the only colored boy in the school.) I made rapid progress, and took great delight in reading and writing. Mr. Mitchell, was very strict with my youthful training, and used to make me read to him one or more chapters in the Bible every Sabbath evening. He also used to have prayers in the family, morning and evening. Thus the four years passed away far more agreeably and pleasantly than the previous nine years. At the expiration of which, I demanded my free papers, feeling that I was now a FREEMAN.

CHAPTER VI.

And now a new era commenced in the history of my life. I soon, subsequently left that section of country, and went to live in the city of Wilmington, Delaware, with Mr. Bringas, a Druggist; he was one of the gentlemen who had previously taken an active part in my liberation. With him I lived some eight months or more; during which time my religious impressions increased, and I availed myself of every opportunity of going to Church.

The many promises that I had made in the earlier part of my life, often occurred to my mind--one of which was, that if I ever lived to be a man, I would serve the Lord. I used to think, when I read that part of the Scriptures which says, "That a man cannot serve two masters," I so understood it, that it meant earthly and divine, and on going to Church one Sunday afternoon, the weather being very pleasant, I stood without the door, listening to the discourse of the Minister, who in the course of his remarks upon the General Judgment, quoted the language of Dr. Watts, which was as follows:

"Look back my soul, look back and wonder!
And see the wicked left behind."

At that moment, my soul became enraptured, and I exclaimed, O! I won't be left behind! and became insensible; on my recovery, I found myself in the sanctuary, amidst the congregation, who were shouting the high praises of God. From that hour I resolved never to stop until I had found the Saviour to be precious to my soul. Shortly after this, I left Wilmington for Philadelphia, where I arrived upon the first Sabbath in August, 1829. Being a stranger, I stopped with a family by the name of Jones, for a few days. After which, I boarded with a family by the name of Herrington, who at that time belonged to the Brick Wesley Church, located in Lombard Street , where I statedly attended religious service; not having as yet experienced pardon of my sins, I left the city and went to Princeton to reside in a Boarding School. There I was taken sick, and soon left. I then journeyed to Trenton, N. J., where I staid the remainder of the winter and engaged in teaching a night school. While there, I joined the church in 1830, under the pastoral charge of the Rev. John Boggs, that sainted father, who has long since laid aside his trumpet in Zion, and has gone home to reap his reward. For more than twenty years have I been a member of the A. M. E. Church--around which, my early affections were thrown, and for its prosperity I have traveled, labored, and endured many privations. My mother before me, sheltered, and fed many of the Fathers, who first entered the field, and cut down the forest, to lay broad its foundation, upon which I have always desired to live and die; but by oppression, and cruel treatment, I have been driven from within its pales. Nevertheless I love the connection, and shall always pray for its prosperity;

because in it I have a great many friends, both Ministers and Laymen, and perhaps a few in whose salvation I have been the humble instrument in the hands of Jesus, of winning over to the kingdom of Grace and Glory.

In the spring of 1831, I left Trenton, New Jersey, for the city of Philadelphia, where for the first time I heard of my mother, whom I had thought was dead. Eighteen years having elapsed since I had either seen or heard of her: this as a matter of course, afforded me unspeakable joy. I immediately sat down and addressed her with a letter. The following is a copy of her letter in reply:

CAROLINA CO. Feb. 3d, 1832.

My Dear Son,

I received your letter on the first day of February, and am very glad to find that you have not forgotten me, and that you think enough of me to write, my dearly beloved son, and I hope that you will continue to do so. I feel very thankful to you, for paying the postage of the letter for me.

My dear Son, I want you to send me something to remember you by. And if you do, send it by Perry Downs, when he comes down, if you please. You say that you are afraid to come--I don't think there will be any danger in your coming now, yet I would be very glad to see you, if you would come down this spring with Perry Downs.

However you can act your pleasure. I sometimes think that I never shall see you again. I feel in hope that I shall; but if I never do, I hope I shall meet you in heaven. There is not a day that I bow before my Maker, but what I bear you up in my petition, that you may hold faithful, till you reach heaven. You wrote me that brother William Richardson is dead; (who was one of the Fathers, who first entered the field, cut down the forest, to lay the foundation of the A. M. E. Church, in the State of Maryland.) I am very sorry for him but the Lord's will be done. I saw your brother about three weeks ago; he was well--I think if he holds out faithful, he will get to heaven. For every time he comes to see me, he sings and prays with me, and for me.

The following is a verse or two of the hymn he usually sang:

> And must I be to judgment brought,
> And answer in that day,
> For every vain and idle thought,
> And every word I say.

> Yes every secret of my heart,
> Shall shortly be made known,
> And I receive my just deserts
> For all that I have done.

We are all well--I want you to write to me soon. Dont let this be the last. Whenever you write pay the postage, as it is difficult for me to get money to pay it. You must write me, if you are married. Adieu, my dear son, and God bless you, are the prayers of

Your affectionate Mother,

SIDNEY ROTTER.

My religious impressions had not left me, but had greatly increased. About this time I tied the nuptial knot with Miss Isabella Lee; she was of a very respectable family. She lived but five weeks and one day, after our celebrating the nuptial feast. She was the object of my earthly regard. The ruthless hand of Death, disregarding my affections, soon snatched her from my embraces-- severing the tender chord of our affections. I now felt that I was bereaved of all that I held sacred and dear to me upon earth. She had previously made no profession to religion, but it pleased the Lord to impart unto her the pardon of her sins, in view of which she sank in the arms of death, with peaceful smiles upon her brow, bidding the world adieu. Some few weeks after her death, I broke up housekeeping, and went to board. With the loss of my dear companion, and the conviction of sin, I was weighed down with sorrow like a cart beneath its shafts. On my way to class, on a Monday evening, I called to see the family who still resided where I removed from, in Elizabeth street, Philadelphia. That family was very pious; the old lady and her daughter were devoted Christians; they were members of the same church and class with myself. While sitting with them conversing upon the subject of religion, I for the first time in my life, secured the evidence of my acceptance with the Saviour. O! that was the happiest hour that I have ever experienced in all the days of my life; from that day until this, I have been striving for the kingdom. I felt I was a sinner saved by Grace.

APPENDIX

Of several Letters, written during my association with the A. M. E. Church upon various subjects touching the social and religious elevation of the Colored People, for whose welfare I have always felt a deep interest. To the Editor of the African Methodist Episcopal Church Magazine.

PHILADELPHIA, Feb. 4, 1844.

REV. GEO. HOGARTH,

Dear Sir--In looking over the tenth number of your valuable Magazine, I there find communications of our beloved brethren, from various parts of our wide spreading connection, touching various subjects, with which I am highly gratified, under page 256 of the last number; also under page 241, that brother D. A. Payne in giving his views in relation to the subject of inspiration, has met with a warm, candid, and scriptural opposition by the Rev. William Moore and Charles Burch. Though I believe brother Payne's motives are for the general good of the present ministry, his post of labor in this city has been of deep interest to some, while it has been opposed by others. Some for the truth of his assertions are searching the Scriptures to know whether the remarks made by him in proof of his doctrines advanced, are scriptural, and also enquiring what did our Lord mean when he told his disciples that it was expedient for them that he should go away, and if he went not away the comforter would not come. Also in John 14: 26, "But the comforter, which is the Holy Ghost, whom the Father will send in my name, he shall teach you all things, and bring all things to your remembrance, whatsoever I have said unto you." In this text we see and have reason to believe that inspiration means an infusing of supernatural ideas.

If this is not the spirit by which men are influenced, I am somewhat at a stand to know. I would ask, is it revelation, or by what spirit is it? We find that revelation is a communication of sacred truths, by a teacher from heaven; and this was given to John on the island of Patmos. Now I wish that some good brother would reconcile those two great points, and let the Church know, so that she maybe able to steer a correct course. Romans 8: 1, 26, 27; Gal. 4: 6, "And because ye are sons, God has sent forth the spirit of his Son into your hearts, crying Abba Father." Ephesians 1: 9, 10, and 14. "Which is the earnest of our inheritance until the redemption of the purchased possession, unto the praise of his glory." Mark 16: 20, "And they went forth and preached everywhere, the Lord working with them, and confirming the word with signs following. Amen." Thus it becomes us who are laborers in the vineyard of the Lord, unto whom precious souls are looking for instructions to thoroughly understand such important points of doctrine. And, in conclusion, I would say that it is by the influence and light of the Holy Comforter, who was promised to the apostles, that the present ministry is assisted in carrying the sacred truths of the Gospel, to the hearts of poor, guilty offending sinners.

Yours for an enlightened ministry,

LEVIN TILMON.

From the African Methodist Episcopal Church Magazine.

A SERMON.

II. Corinth. iv. 17.--For our light affliction, which is but for a moment worketh for us a far more exceeding and eternal weight of glory. * * *, For we know that if our earthly house of this tabernacle were dissolved, we have a building of God, a house not made with hands, eternal in the heavens; * * * * * and for me to live is Christ; and to die is gain.

If there were neither punishment nor torment after this life to be feared, the wicked and unbelievers who prosper in the world might esteem themselves the happiest of men; and if there were neither glory nor rewards to be expected after death, the righteous and the faithful, who drink cups full of bitterness and sorrow here below, would be miserable. But if we search and examine the sacred records we shall find more difference between heaven and earth, between light and darkness; and if we look at the ultimate fate of the wicked and unbelievers, we shall find that death deprives them not only of their honors, riches, treasures and carnal enjoyments in this life, but are become forever lost in a vast sea of bitterness and sorrow. If death relieves their bodies from temporary afflictions, under which all the children of Adam are more or less circumstanced, yet it casts their souls into eternal torments of spiritual wretchedness. To the virtuous and believing Christian, death is a great friend, it delivers them from many evils and miseries in this life, and opens to them the gate that leads to endless glory and happiness. Our Saviour endeavored to persuade us of this truth in that remarkable parable of the 15th chapter of St. Luke. On one hand he shows a rich miser clothed in purple and fine linen, feeding upon dainties and living in splendor, and on the other hand he discovers to us a poor man covered with sores, lying at the rich man's gate, entreating that he might share with the dogs in the crumbs that fell from his table, but without success. At length the poor man died and was carried by angels into Abraham's bosom. O, wonderful change! he that lately was scarce good enough for the company of dogs is now in the bosom of Abraham, where he can enjoy himself in angels embraces, and is fed with the bread of the living God. The rich man died also, but whilst his body was laid in the earth with great honor, the devils dragged his soul into hell and cast it into a fire that burns continually--a fire that nothing is able to extinguish. The poor man that was a beggar at his gate, is now required to dip the tip of his finger in water and cool the gentleman's tongue while suffering the vengeance of heaven in burning torments. St. Paul informs us that as many have sinned without law shall perish without law, but they that profess to know the law shall be judged by the law. Such as have already heard the thunders of Mount Sinai and will not humble themselves, shall one day feel the thunderbolts of majestic wrath, which will cause them to know, by dreadful experience, what it is to rebel against God. They will draw down upon their guilty heads the terrible curses of his law, for cursed be he that confirmeth not all the words of this law to do them. There are no people in the world who have cause to expect a more rigorous sentence and dreadful punishment, than wicked Christians. Those who profess to know God and believe in Jesus Christ, yet deny him by their works and trample under foot the riches of his grace! can such imagine that after having had the gospel preached to them, and seen Jesus Christ crucified as it were, before their eyes, and yet have profited nothing thereby, expect to be ultimately happy? Surely not. I here sincerely advise those, who with so much ease, often arrange many essential passages of Scriptures, in order to bend them to suit their purposes, to beware and desist, lest they be found fighting against God: for cursed be he that shall add or diminish aught to or from the sacred Scriptures. A passage in Luke, 12th ch. 47--48, deserves particular consideration. Here that servant which knows his Lord's will, and prepared not himself, nor did according to his will, shall be beaten with many stripes;

but he that knows not and did commit things worthy of stripes, shall be beaten with few; for unto whomsoever much is given, of him shall much be required, and to whom men have committed much, of him they will ask the more. Some from this text conclude that if they keep themselves ignorant of the will of their Maker, or of his command, and live a mere moral life, that their stripes will be so few that their punishment will be but trifling, and that it will be immaterial whether they get to heaven or not. This negligent disposition in man is exemplified by thousands in our day. They live as if they thought there was no benefit to be derived by living a religious life. Our Saviour was directing his discourse to his ministers in the passage of Scripture we have just noticed, urging them to pay attention to their charge, and if they did not they should be beaten with many stripes. I think he meant that they should experience a smitten countenance in this life, according to the talent given. He that is faithful to improve his talent, whether great or small, shall have a full reward in the other world. We read further, that he who breaks one of the least of the commandments, shall be guilty of the whole. We must infer from this text that the punishment will be for the violation of the whole of the commandments. Some also inquire, whether in paradise there shall be an equality or inequality of glory and happiness? This question is more curious than necessary; for without puzzling our heads whether they shall be any more or less happy than ourselves, it is sufficient for our comfort to know, that if we truly believe, and are penitent, if we fear God as we ought, and serve Him religiously to the end of our lives, we shall certainly attain to the glory of the children of God, and possess with them a perfect and eternal happiness. Some believe that in paradise there shall be but one glory and happiness, which shall be equal and uniform in all believers, and that as our Divine Saviour hath purchased this glory and happiness for all the elect equally, so they shall all enjoy it in the highest degree of perfection. Secondly, our Saviour saith expressly, without any exceptions, that the righteous shall shine forth, as the sun, in the kingdom of their Father. Thirdly, Jesus Christ represents to us the transactions that shall take place at the end of the world, by the parable of a house-holder who went out early in the morning to hire laborers into his vineyard, who, when even was come, gave the same hire unto every one that labored in his vineyard, though some of them had labored but one hour; some complained, and he said unto them, is it not lawful for me to do what I will with mine own; is thine eye evil because I am good? So the last shall be first and the first last, for many be called, but few chosen.--Matt. 20th ch. Others think, on the contrary, that in heaven there shall be an inequality of glory and divers degrees of happiness. Thus they chiefly rest their faith upon that passage of the Holy Scripture which we find in John 14 ch. 2 v., where Christ said to his apostles, in my Father's house are many mansions. He doth not say or add, that some of them are richer and more glorious than others, but only, "in my Father's house are many mansions." Now those who cannot reconcile themselves with the belief of an equality of glory and happiness, because they think they are entitled to something more than common, let such be careful, lest they should seem to envy poor Lazarus, who is now in Abraham's bosom. As for my part, I shall think myself sufficiently happy, if I am admitted to be his companion in paradise. Some inquire whether the souls of the righteous, when they leave this earthly tabernacle, doth ascend into heaven as soon as it hath left the body. According to what our Saviour promised to the crucified thief, it will enter into a blissful state: "Verily I say unto thee, this day thou shalt be with me in Paradise." Luke 23 ch. Our blessed Saviour entered into heaven both in soul and body after his resurrection. St. Stephen declared, when he cried out, "I see the heavens open, and Jesus Christ sitting at the right hand of God." Acts 7th ch. It is also inquired whether the souls of the damned go down immediately after their exit from the body, and are tormented in an unquenchable flame, as we learn by the Christian religion, particularly by the parable of the rich glutton. We understand, through that passage of Scripture, that these wretches are already judged. How is it, then, that the Son of God will judge them again at the last day, and condemn them to an everlasting fire, prepared for the devil and his angels. I answer, when the souls of the wicked depart out of their wretched bodies, God pronounces to them the sentence of their condemnation. Before the resurrection the soul alone feels the effect of that sentence. But when Jesus Christ shall sit upon the throne of his glory, then shall both soul and body be cast into everlasting fire. From this we may understand that there are three degrees of punishment or torments to the wicked. In this life they have a kind of hell that racks their guilty consciences. At their going out of the world their souls are plunged into eternal flames; their bodies, in the meantime, are as insensible in their graves as the bodies of the righteous. But at this last and dreadful day of judgment, their souls shall be again united to their miserable bodies to suffer the pangs of an eternal death. Some inquire, what shall become of this elemental world? whether the heavens and the earth, which sustain us, shall perish, or whether they shall remain after the great day of the coming of our Lord. I answer, the Scriptures assure us, that the world shall totally perish, as God hath made the heavens and the earth out of nothing, He will reduce them all again into their primitive state, and intends to create others more beautiful, more holy, and far more glorious. There are several expressions that favor this opinion: St. Peter in his 2d epistle, 3d. chap., gives us the most clear account of this. He says the heavens shall pass away with a noise, and the elements shall melt with heat, and the earth with the works that are therein shall be burnt up. Nevertheless, we, according to His promise, look for new heavens and a new earth, wherein dwelleth righteousness. St. John adds, Seeing then that all these things shall be dissolved, what manner of persons ought ye to be in all holy conversation and godliness? There is no man, who is a real Christian, can doubt that wonderful change which shall happen to the world at the last day. The heavens and the earth are not pure in the sight of God, who requires a resurrection of the dead bodies of mankind. This being so generally acknowledged, it will not be necessary to say much on that subject. To maintain that the resurrection of the body is impossible, or will not take place, is the most extravagant atheism; it is impudently denying the infinite power of God and the sacred history of the creation of the world. For if we believe that God fashioned Eve out of one of Adam's ribs; that he made Adam of the dust, and that he created that dust out of nothing, canst thou not as readily believe that God is able, in the day of the resurrection, to rebuild the body out of the dust into which it is reduced by death. If thou believest that God breathed into Adam's nostrils the breath of life, that He created the soul and placed it into the body, where it never was before, how canst thou question His power of returning, in one day, the same soul into the same body, where it formerly abode? It may be asked, with what stature of body shall the dead arise? I answer, the righteous body arise again in what may be called a perfect stature of body, without deficiency or infirmity. Some may be disposed farther to enquire, what bodies the wicked shall have at and after the resurrection. If we consider the smoke of the bottomless pit, the fury of the infernal flames, with the violent torments which the wicked shall suffer, perhaps we might conclude, they shall appear ill-favored, deformed, and dreadful to behold; that there will appear in their guilty looks and ghastly countenances, the image of Satan and the furies of hell. But be this as it will, the bodies of the wicked will be immortal, and their immortality a miserable one; and that it had been better for them had they never been born, rather than thus live to die eternally--to be ever dying, yet never dead. We know, that whatever God hath appointed in His eternal counsel, must be fulfilled in time, and all things in the world attain those ends for which He made them, and since he created our souls not to be alone, but to exist with the body, it follows that this body which is cast down by death, must needs be renewed and raised again at the resurrection, that the soul may return to it and dwell with it forever. The digestive powers of man and beast, and the decay of nature seem to preclude the idea that God will give himself the trouble to raise the same body at the last day, when he can make its kindred dust answer the same purpose, that he will sift a great part of the earth, in order to collect all the particles that had formed the several bodies of the human family, and also pass, as through a strainer, the whole waters of the sea for the above purpose; and then, after separating them, unite their kindred particles, so as to be able to form the self-same body. I do not dispute His power to do this, for I believe that Jesus Christ is able to speak into life the bodies of all the human family which are crumbled into dust, as readily as he did that of Lazarus, which had been four days dead and buried.--John, chap. 11. But I hardly think he will take this round-about way, to collect the ruins of our corrupt bodies and restore them to their former condition. It is well known that the bodies of men are often devoured by fish and other animals, which are eaten by man, and there are nations which feed upon human flesh. Now all these bodies undergo a fermentation, are digested, and assist in forming other bodies; and were we (v. 2) to receive again the old bodies thus crumbled into the dust, at the resurrection, as they must first be made up new bodies, it would be a contradiction in itself to call them old. To collect the shattered pieces of an old building and put them up in the form of a building, would be putting up a new house, although the materials were from an old one. Are we not told that we must put off the old man and put on the new man, which, after God, is created in righteousness and true holiness? Eph. chap. 4. The best thing we can say of this house of earth is, that it is a ruinous building, and will not be long before it tumbles into dust; that it is not our home, we look for another house eternal in the heavens. As our bodies shall return to their mother earth, it cannot possibly make any difference to us whether the bodies which we shall be clothed with on the last day, are made of the same old materials, or of its kindred earth, or of the new earth, which shall be made at that time, as it cannot add anything to the glory and happiness of our souls or bodies. Neither has it been revealed to us whether the resurrection is to take place before the earth is burnt up, or at the time, or at the forming of the new earth. I therefore think it labor lost, for ministers of the Gospel to occupy too much of their time, as some do, in describing the ability of God to search out and collect these millions of millions of old shattered bodies, and restore them again to their several owners. This difficulty must only tend to puzzle the minds of their hearers, and raise doubts in their minds, and thereby shake their faith respecting the truth of other passages of Scripture which would be far better for them to understand. We know that there are many passages of Scripture which cannot be well understood in their literal meaning, and are only typical, and intended to rouse our minds up to understand that something extraordinary will take place, or must be done. Our blessed Lord has ordered that the souls of men, at the last day, shall again be clothed with bodies as at first, for a wise purpose. For what can that be? Why, undoubtedly, to increase the glory and happiness of the saints, and also to swell the torments of the damned. St. Peter in his 2d epistle, 3d chap., tells us that we are to look for new heavens and a new earth, wherein dwelleth righteousness. May we not then conclude from this, that this new earth will become a new garden of Eden, and will be peopled with saints? Such men, for instance, as Adam was before his fall; and, as in that case, they will need bodies as at first, and perhaps can as fully enjoy themselves in this new garden, as Adam did in the old one. O! would it not be the height of wisdom for us to secure to ourselves this happiness? Certainly our salvation is a matter of too much importance to be neglected; our life too uncertain to admit of delay; and our souls too precious to run the hazard of losing them. Had we many souls we might venture the loss of one, but seeing that we have but one only, and that if it be lost, all the riches and treasures of the world cannot redeem it, we should watch day and night for its preservation. We should be seized with a holy dread, and carefully avoid whatsoever might cast our precious soul into the second death and everlasting damnation. This is what our blessed Savior invites and exhorts us to. "Watch:" saith he, "For ye know not what hour your Lord doth come." Matt. ch. 24 v. 42. "Watch and pray, that ye enter not into temptation." ch. 26 v. 41. This exhortation is so necessary that he often repeats it. Take ye heed, watch and pray, for ye know not when the time is; for as a snare shall it come on all them that dwell on the face of the whole earth; watch ye therefore, and pray always that ye may be accounted worthy to escape all these things that shall come to pass, and stand before the Son of God, there to be happy forever.

Soon as from earth I go,
What will become of me?
Eternal happiness or woe,
Must then my portion be.

Thou art thyself the way,
Thyself in me reveal,
So shall I spend my life's short day,
Obedient to thy will.

L. T.

PORT JEFFERSON, N. Y., Nov. 22d; 1844.

Rev. George Hogarth:--Dear Sir; I now forward this communication to you, hoping you will give it a notice in your valuable Magazine.

Since I have been in this section of the country, so far as my mission is concerned, I find the colored population very scattering and very much uncultivated for the want of the light of the Gospel and its influence. Though scattering, I find they manifest a great desire to have the Bible and its declarations made manifest unto them by their colored brethren. There are some who belong among the white Methodists and Presbyterians, but they would rather unite with their own people. It becomes our duty to cast our lot with them, that we may be the better able to prove a blessing to them. A few days ago, I received an invitation to preach for my white brethren, at a place called Stony Brook, and on my way thither, I was invited to call at the cottage of a lonely Indian squaw, with one little female child. The cottage stands amid a lonesome wilderness, and while the dreary winds howl through the forest, the aspect throws a deep solemnity on the mind of a weary traveller. And when I entered, I introduced the subject of religion, and strove to impress upon her mind the shortness of time and the great need there was of moral reform. I was informed, that from the early period of her life, she had dragged out a miserable existence, but from the exhortation and prayer, and the small pittance that I was able to leave with her, she manifested a great desire to cast her lot with the people of God. I bade her adieu, and left her, hoping that she, with all connected with her, would meet me in the kingdom of God. Having as I trust, been of some blessing to my fellow-men in those remote parts of L. I., I then left for lands more distant, as I felt it a duty enjoined upon me. As I assure you, my beloved brother, that my desire is, that if I can be of any good to my church and people, my will is to do so.

For the accomplishing of this noble enterprise, I ask the prayers of all them that love Zion, that the great cause of the Redeemer's kingdom may go forward, through my feeble efforts, in distant places where our church has not yet been established, until all those places where our people are enveloped in darkness, may shine forth as a lamp that burneth, and that the time may come when divisions among us may be done away, and the Gospel of the Son of God may rest on the shoulder of his ministers in purity, and they preach it in spirit, might and power. Since I have left my home, I have through the providence of God, travelled more than three hundred miles in less than one month, and labored more than twelve times. On the 23d inst., I left my lodging at one o'clock in the morning, in company with brother J--, Abraham Tobias and others, and went more than forty miles; the most part of our journey was through the wilderness. Just as we got to a place called the Station, we made a kind of a halt, to think on our way, and while standing, we discovered a man running toward us, having on neither hat or coat; we hailed him, and soon found his motives were to put us out of our way that we might fall a prey to himself and his band; but, finding there were six of us in number, he was disappointed in his design. I called to the driver to go forward, he did so, and I am happy to say that we were enabled to escape the device of the villain who might have had a trap laid to ensnare us. We made the place of our destiny a little after sunrise, and there we met with friends and brethren who received us with open arms; among whom, was Rev. E. N. Hall, and brother Edward C. Africanus: we spent the morning with them, and then bid them adieu, and reached our home about 11 o'clock that night. At the above-mentioned place, on our return back, we met six more ruffians, but we past them unmolested, for which we were truly thankful.

Yours, with the highest respect in the bonds of a peaceful gospel,

LEVIN TILMON.

STONINGTON, February 25th, 1845.

REV. GEORGE HOGARTH:

Dear Brother,--This is to inform you that I am well at present, and I hope yourself and family enjoy the same blessing. The work of the Lord is going on with us in

Stonington and Greenport. There are nearly thirty members here, and nearly twenty in Greenport, and we are now making great preparation to build a church. We have something like three hundred and thirty dollars subscribed, and the white citizens say that they will stand by us: and I can truly say that the Lord is with us.

Remember me to brother Robinson and brother E. N. Hall.

Yours in Christ,

L. TILMON.

NORTHWICH, Aug. 6th, 1845.

REV. GEO. HOGARTH:

Dear Sir,--I now write to inform you of the present state of our society. We have been getting along very prosperously, and the people are becoming considerably united. We held our Bush-meeting on the first Sabbath in August, and had a very peaceable time, and sinners wept bitterly. As it regards the house for worship, I have been using all my influence in order to unite the people. I am striving for the general good of the people of this place. On the part of the Methodists, I can truly say, their influence is encouraging. And as the church was closed from Sunday night until Sunday night again, we now have services three times a day. In the afternoons and at nights, we have large congregations. As the house has never been finished, we are trying to do something towards it, and we have succeeded in getting a pulpit up. We however, had scarcely got it finished, before it was taken down by the opposite party; but it was an unprofitable job to them; the steward entered a suit against them, which was taken up in behalf of the State, and postponed until the following Monday. They had to give bonds to the amount of fifty dollars, twenty-five each, in order to get a gentleman to enter bonds for them until the sitting of the court. I think we shall have better days after this, for those are the two men who have always kept up a bad state of feeling among the colored people in this place, and have always done pretty much as they pleased, and have now got into trouble.

Yours, in behalf of the connection,

L. TILMON.

From the A. M. E. Church Magazine.

PROVIDENCE. R. I., July 21, 1847.

REV. GEO. HOGARTH-- Dear Brother: I avail myself of this opportunity to inform you that my health is reasonable at this time, and I hope that this favor may find you safe and sound, enjoying the same blessing of God. I have had quite a vacation since I left conference, owing to the church here undergoing an enlargement and remodelling. It is nearly finished, and will be dedicated on the first Sabbath in August, God willing, at which time and place I would be pleased to see you. The church looks well, and will exceed in dimension any colored church in the city. I wish you to give my best respects to the Rev. J. Matthews, and inform him that a word or two from his pen would be cordially received. You will please inform me when and where your next camp meeting will be held.

Yours in Christ,

L. TILMON.

From the *Roman Citizen.*

An Eulogy from the pen of Rev. N. W. Knox, Pastor of the first Presbyterian Church of Rome, New York, March, 1849, on Laying the Corner Stone of the A. M. E. Church.

Agreeably to the usages of the African M. E. Church, the ceremony of laying the corner stone of the new Church for the colored people of this place, is to take place on Tuesday, the 9th inst., at 2 o'clock, P. M.

One design of this ceremony is to interest the citizens of this village in this attempt to promote the good of our colored population, by affording them a proof that the new enterprise is in progress, and likely to succeed.

The writer of this notice feels that it is but an act of justice to our neglected colored population, that a proper sympathy with them in this attempt should be manifested by the citizens at large. The Rev. Mr. Tilmon, their pastor, is a man of decided energy of character, whose motto is, "never to fail" in anything he undertakes. He has already succeeded beyond the expectation of all his friends, and if life and health is spared, there is now no reasonable doubt of a triumphant result.

Too great value cannot be attached to the efforts he is making among us in behalf of his own people, not only by his labors in preaching the Gospel, but by affording them the example of one of their own number, who by earnest industry, and steady perseverance, has risen to a highly respectable standing as a man of intelligence; to the accumulation of a pecuniary competence and to a useful position as a Minister of Christ.

Let the people of this place be willing to encourage him in his self-denying and arduous efforts, and rest assured he will not disappoint the trust reposed in him.

This hasty notice is written, it may be proper to state, without the solicitation of Mr. Tilmon.

From the *Christian Herald.*

NEW BEDFORD, Mass. Oct. 27, 1848.

REV. A. R. GREEN:

Dear Brother,--I have just received the first, second and third numbers of the "Christian Herald," which I hail with pleasure, as a welcome messenger to the shores of New England, bearing as it does, good news to all; the dead are alive, and the lost are found. And may we not say as one of old, "Rejoice not O mine enemy, though I fall, yet will I arise." I had almost despaired of your success, but I feel that the clouds are breaking, it is passing over: the light is appearing, and the day begins to dawn.

I have made some efforts to obtain subscribers, but I have met with very little success as yet. One reason is, that our people here, are generally poor, and having a large debt to contend with, they have been much straightened, during the summer and fall, in order to make a payment of one hundred dollars which was promptly met, on the 16th of this month. Having accomplished that, I shall turn my attention more fully to the Book Concern, in order to obtain subscribers and to raise the two cent money.

L. TILMON.

From the *Roman Citizen*.

NEW YORK, May, 1850.

Third Report of the Agent of A. M. E. Church of Rome, in Canal Village.

The undersigned, who has, since the 14th of January last, acted as Agent in collecting funds for the purpose of erecting a house for Religious Worship, for the colored people of this place, takes this method of returning his sincere thanks to the benevolent citizens for their timely assistance and encouragement in the undertaking. The edifice is now up, and nearly finished, and will be a neat and comfortable house when completed. The progress of the enterprise, thus far, seems to have given general satisfaction, and its completion will doubtless prove a great benefit to the colored people of Rome. We feel much indebted to the clergymen of this place for their kindness in aiding us by their liberal subscriptions and influence. We feel no less grateful to the Hon. S. B. Roberts, E. Huntington, Dr. J. V. Cobb, L. Abell, Hon. H. A. Foster, and many others, who have been friends to us in time of need.

In justice to our feelings, we cannot close these remarks without noticing the untiring efforts that some of the ladies are making in visiting from house to house, distributing their charities among the poor children and preparing them for the Sabbath School room--the nursery of the Christian Churches.

The amount that has been received from the citizens of Rome and the Ridge, in cash and materials, is $187. Leaving a balance on subscription, unpaid, of $38.

The total amount received from citizens residing in other places, was $118.11.

L. TILMON.

From the *Roman Citizen.*

NEW YORK, Oct. 20, 1849.

The Settlers on Smith's Land in Oneida County.

At a Meeting of the Colored Emigrants held upon the Smith lands in Florence, Oneida Co., N. Y., at the Emigrant House, on Saturday, October 20th, 1849, Rev. D. Peterson, General Agent, was present, and made a statement of the amount of money received by him as donations for the Association, and of the following named articles:--

First, a box of very useful Books, suitable for a Sabbath School Library, together with other useful articles, presented by C. Whipple, Esq., of Newburyport, Mass. Second, a Plow and Pitchfork, presented by E. Bartlet, Esq., of the same place. Third, one Shovel and Pitchfork, presented by Mr. Brown, of Gardiner, Maine.-- Fourth, a bag of very useful articles, presented by Mr. P Wadsworth, of Bath, Maine, (a gift in part from the Ladies.) After receiving the above named donations, it was on motion.

Resolved, That we, the Emigrants of the Florence Settlement, tender our sincere thanks to the above named gentlemen, and citizens, generally, and also to the General Agent, for his efforts to render assistance to the Settlement, until we shall have passed the first winter in our newly acquired homes, having arrived so late at the settlement, that we could not realize a sufficient crop to sustain us during the approaching winter.

We also take pleasure in saying that we found the white citizens of Florence to be a kind and generous hearted people, who bid us welcome upon our arrival in their midst, and extended to us the hand of brotherly love: and we can enjoy our individual rights in the midst of such a people, which are life, liberty and the pursuit of happiness. We take pleasure in saying that the anti-slavery spirit is developing in the bosoms of many of the citizens of Florence and its vicinity, and we give with pleasure the names of some with whom we have become acquainted. Rev. Mr. Garland, Rev. Benj. Fuller, Mr. Trimbal, Mr. Richards, Mr. Smith, Mr. Sparrow and family, and many others.

Florence village is 22 miles from the village of Rome, by way of Taberg, and we have always found it very pleasant and agreeable in travelling that road, and we take pleasure in recommending the respectable portion of the travelling public, irrespective of color, to favor Mr. Hyde, of Taberg, with their patronage. They will find his accommodations good, the House large, neat, and well regulated, and himself and lady very agreeable. And as they proceed on to Florence village they will find Mr. Fairbanks, also very much of a gentleman, who keeps a good House, and pays every attention to the travelling public. We cannot close without making mention of the citizens of Rome. We have found them to be an enterprising and benevolent community, and we feel grateful to them for past favors. We are also indebted to the proprietors of the Roman Citizen, for favors received.

The Settlement is also particularly indebted to D. G. Dorrance, Esq., of Florence, for his kindness to the settlers, and his exertions to promote the interests of the Association.

We would say that the prospects of the Settlement are favorable, and that we intend to give a general statement of its affairs through the columns of the public Newspapers as soon as practicable.

D. MACCOY, President.

W HAWKINS, Secretary.

L. TILMON, in behalf of the Society.

NEW BEDFORD, March, 22, 1848.

FREDERICK DOUGLASS:--I became a subscriber to the North Star when it was first established. I was induced to do so, because its prospectus met my views. I shall continue to take it as long as it continues to attack slavery in all its forms, and aims to hasten the day of emancipation.

I believe there are various means by which the bondman's liberation may be brought about, and the condition of the nominally free colored people materially bettered. It becomes you and me, and all others who feel for the oppressed, with whom we are identified, to use all moral energies to wipe out the foul stain of American slavery. Though our means are various, let our aims be the same. Let us not fall out by the way, as did the Israelites in the deserts, lest our selfish dissensions bring down upon us like sufferings.

In looking over the North Star of Dec. 22d, I saw a communication, headed "New Settlement." I read it with deep interest, and at once entered into the spirit of the communication. I was glad to see such an enterprise as the Florence Association started as announced in the communication. I was also glad to see your name, with the names of many other leading colored men of this country, associated with the enterprise, as approvers of it. I was not acquainted with several of these gentlemen, except by reputation. Their names were sufficient to secure for the Florence enterprise my confidence.

In the North Star of March 16th, I was surprised and sorry to see a letter of yours, in which you request your name to be erased as one of the inspectors of public works, as desiring to have nothing more to do with the enterprise, and this in consequence of reports that have been put in circulation. I wish you had told us what those reports were.

Now, friend Douglass, I believe the Florence enterprise to be sound, inside and out--thoroughly anti-slavery in its spirit and tendency. And so I believe the gift of three thousand deeds to the colored inhabitants of the State of New York, is a great anti-slavery act, characteristic of that noble man, Gerrit Smith. It will be long cherished in the hearts of the colored people of this country, and particularly by those living in the State of New York. You will see that persons living in other States could not participate in that rich gift, though they rejoiced at it. When the Florence enterprise was started by our friend, Stephen Myers, and others, put before the public under such favorable auspices, many very respectable colored people, living in the surrounding States, were induced to make purchases. They knew that if they went to the Smith lands they must purchase them.

I do not pretend to be well acquainted with the geography of the State of New York: but in looking over the map of that State, I see that Florence and Oneida county are situated in the central part of the State, while Franklin and Essex are in the North-eastern part--Franklin extending to Canada on the North. Franklin and Essex counties appear to be comparatively isolated, thinly populated, and out of the great highways and facilities for transporting products or persons to and from the State difficult. According to the map before me of the State of New York in 1840, Franklin county contained 16,580 inhabitants, and Essex county contained 23,634. Since

1840, the number has no doubt increased; nor is there any doubt that the same is true of Oneida county.

According to the same map, Oneida county is near the centre of the State. Both the Erie Canal and Railroad pass through this county. Facilities for the transportation of produce or persons are superior. It is a populous county. In 1840, it contained a population of 85,310, more than double the number contained both in Franklin and Essex counties. Then look at its large and flourishing towns, such as Utica, Rome, Clinton, Whitesboro, &c. Florence, the proposed settlement, is in this county. In view of the considerations presented, it seems to me that the lands in Florence, Oneida county, are the most valuable--that they are preferable to those who wish to purchase.

Our friend Stephen Myers informed us that Gerrit Smith had given to several colored people lands in Florence; that he was one of those persons. He felt desirous of doing something to better the condition of his people. Accordingly, himself and several other gentlemen, Grantees of the Smith land in Florence agreed to put their lands together. Other lands were purchased from Gerrit Smith's agent, by Mr. Myers, in behalf of this company of gentlemen. This company now propose to establish a settlement at Florence, for the purpose of farming, dealing in lumber, manufacturing potash, and practising the various trades, and thus raising themselves in public estimation.

If Mr. Myers has purchased these lands, and met his contracts, and I believe he has, (in testimony of which, Mr. Gerrit Smith informed me in a note, that he had received a letter from Mr. Myers, stating that he [Mr. Myers] had deposited in bank $73.00 to the credit of the Florence land purchased of his [Mr. Smith's] agent,) why should those who are not disposed to favor the Florence enterprise, throw obstacles in its way? It seems to me something more than mere suspicion. Unauthenticated reports are required to justify such a course; and yet these are all that (it would seem) can be put forth by those who are unfriendly to the Florence enterprise.

It is said that the country is a wilderness; that its settlement will be attended with difficulties; that colored people are not accustomed to hardships, &c., &c. Our forefathers, have made this country, once a wilderness, a delightful home for their oppressors, the Anglo-Saxon race. We, their offspring, to this day are "hewers of wood and drawers of water," degraded, crushed beneath public sentiment and popular religion.

Henry Clay and his coadjutors, who are looked up to as the giants in this nation, are still using their power to keep us down, still determined to drive us out of this country--still determined to colonize us to Africa. But this is our country, the soil on which we were born. Here are our homes. Let us build ourselves up by all righteous means. Let us cherish no divisions among ourselves. United we stand, divided we fall.

Yours for the good cause of the Elevation and Improvement of our people.

LEVIN TILMON.

To Captain Thomas Auld, formerly my Master.

No. 4 ALEXANDER-ST., ROCHESTER,
September 3d, 1849.

DEAR SIR:--I propose to celebrate this, the 11th anniversary of my escape from your dominion, by addressing to you a friendly epistle on the subject of slavery.

I do this partly with a view to the fulfillment of a promise I made you on this day one year ago, and partly to neutralize certain charges which I then brought against you.

Ungrateful and unjust as you, perhaps, deem me, I should despise myself if I could willfully malign the character even of a slaveholder; and if, at any time, I have appeared to you guilty of such conduct, you have greatly misapprehended me. I can say, with a clear conscience, in all that I have ever written or spoken respecting yourself, I have tried to remember that, though I am beyond your power and control, I am still accountable to our common Father and Judge, in the sight of whom I believe that I stand acquitted of all intentional misrepresentation against you. Of course, I have said many hard things respecting yourself; but all has been based upon what I knew of you at the time I was a slave in your family. Of the past, therefore, I have nothing to take back; but information concerning you and your household, lately received, makes it unjust and unkind for me to continue the style of remark, in regard to your character, which I primarily adopted. I have been told by a person intimately acquainted with your affairs, and upon whose word I can rely, that you have ceased to be a slaveholder, and have emancipated all your slaves, except my poor old grandmother, who is now too old to sustain herself in freedom; and that you have taken her from the desolate hut in which she formerly lived, into your own kitchen, and are now providing for her in a manner becoming a man and a Christian.

This, sir, is indeed good news; and is all the more gratifying to me, since it deprives the pro-slavery public of the North of what they deem a powerful argument against me, and the abolitionists generally. It proves that the agitation of the subject of slavery does not hinder, if it does not help, the emancipation of slaves at the South. I have been frequently told that my course would have an unfavorable influence upon the condition of my friends and relatives in your possession; and the common argument against abolitionists may be stated as follows: Let slaveholders alone, and they will emancipate their slaves; and that agitation only retards the progress of the slave's liberation. It is alleged that the slaveholder is induced to clutch more firmly what is attempted to be wrested from him. To this argument your case is a plain contradiction. If the effect of anti-slavery agitation were such as is thus alleged, you would have been among the first to have experienced it: for few slaveholders in this land have had a larger share of public exposure and denunciation than yourself; and this, too, from a quarter most calculated to annoy, and to provoke resentment. All this, however, has not prevented you from nobly discharging the high duty you owed alike to God and to the slaves in your possession. I congratulate you warmly, and I rejoice most sincerely, that you have been able, against all the suggestions of self-interest, of pride, and of love of power, to perform this act of pure justice and humanity. It has greatly increased my faith in man, and in the latent virtue even of slaveholders. I say latent virtue, not because I think slaveholders are worse than all other men, but because, such are the power and influence of education and habit upon even the best constituted minds, that they paralyze and disorder, if not destroy their moral energy: and of all persons in the world, slaveholders are in the most unfavorable position for retaining their power. It would be easy for me to give you the reason of this, but you may be presumed to know it already.

Born and brought up in the presence and under the influence of a system which at once strikes at the very foundation of morals by denying--if not the existence of God--the equal brotherhood of mankind, by degrading one part of the human family to the condition of brutes, and by reversing all right ideas of justice and of brotherly kindness, it is almost impossible that one so environed can greatly grow in virtuous rectitude.

You, however, sir, have risen superior to these unhallowed influences, and have added another striking proof to those already existing, that the heart of the slaveholder is still within the reach of the truth, and that to preach to him the duty of letting "the oppressed go free," is not in vain.

I shall no longer regard you as an enemy to freedom, nor to myself--but shall hail you as a friend to both. Before doing so, however, I have one reasonable request to make of you, with which you will, I hope, comply. It is this: That you make your conversion to anti-slavery known to the world, by precept as well as by example. A publication of the facts relating to the emancipation of your slaves, with reasons that have led you to this humane act, would doubtless prove highly beneficial to the cause of freedom generally--at the same time that it would place yourself in that high estimation of the public mind to which your generous conduct justly entitles you. I think you have no right to put your candle under a bushel. Your case is different in many respects from that of most repentant slaveholders. You have been publicly and peculiarly exposed before the world for being a slaveholder; and since you have ceased to be such, a just regard for your own standing among men, as well as a desire to promote the happiness of a deeply injured people, require you to make known your sentiments on this important subject.--It would be truly an interesting and a glorious spectacle to see master and slave, hand in hand, laboring together for the overthrow of American slavery. I am sure that such an example would tell with thrilling effect upon the public mind of this section. We have already had the example of slaves and slaveholders, side by side, battling for freedom; but we yet lack a master working by the side of his former slave on the anti-slavery platform. You have it in your power to supply this deficiency; and if you can bring yourself to do so, you will attain a larger degree of happiness for yourself, and will confer a greater blessing on the cause of freedom than that you have already done by the generous act of emancipating your own slaves. With the example before me, I shall not despair of yet having the pleasure of giving you the right hand of fellowship on the anti-slavery platform.

Before closing the present letter, I wish to set you right about a matter which is, perhaps, of small importance to yourself, but is of considerable consequence to me.

In your letter, written three years ago, to Mr. A. C. C. Thompson, of Wilmington, respecting the validity of my narrative, you complained that I failed to mention your intention to emancipate me at the age of twenty-five. The reason of this failure is as follows: You will remember that your promise to emancipate me preceded my first attempt to escape; and that you then told me that you would have emancipated me, had I not made the attempt in question. If you ask me why I distrusted your promise in the first instance, I could give you many reasons; but the one that weighed most with me was the passage of a law in Maryland, throwing obstructions in the way of emancipation; and I had heard you refer to that law as an excuse for continuing your slaves in bondage: and, supposing the obstructions alluded to might prove insuperable barriers to my freedom, I resolved upon flight, as the only alternative left me short of a life of slavery. I hope that this explanation will be satisfactory. I do not regret what I have done--but rather rejoice in it, as well for your sake as mine. Nevertheless, I wish to be fairly understood, and have, therefore, made the explanation.

I shall here conclude this letter by again expressing my sincere gratitude at the magnanimous deed with which your name is now associated--and by repeating the ardent hope that you will publicly identify yourself with the holy cause of freedom, to which, since I left your service, I have been most unremittingly devoting myself.

I am Dear Sir,
Very respectfully yours,

FREDERICK DOUGLASS.

HYMN.

O, if poor sinners did but know
How much for them I undergo,
They would not treat me with contempt,
Nor curse me when I say REPENT.
Give credit now to what I say,
And mind it till the judgment day:
Of God I'm sent, constrained to go,
To call upon both high and low:
And wo is me if I refrain
From going forth in God's great name.
A dispensation I've received,
And my kind friends, I now must leave,
My father's house I bid adieu,
And on my journey now pursue:
To distant climes I now repair,
To call poor sinners far and near:
But O! the trials of my heart
To think I must with parents part;
In tears I leave them all in grief,
I cannot give to them relief:
They brought me up with tender care,
And for my health no pains they'd spare--
Expos'd themselves by night and day,
Whilst fevers wore my flesh away.
My loving brethren think it strange
That I do not return again:
Through beating winds of rain and snow,

Both wet and cold, I have to go
To 'tend the appointments I have made,
And find a place to lay my weary head.
I draw no pension here below
To pay my charges as I go:
I go forth on my own expense,
And trust in God for my defense:
Oft times with hunger I grow faint,
And travel on till almost spent:
I find no friend nor helper nigh,
But him who hears the ravens cry:
Oft times I with false brethren meet,
Whose hearts are fill'd with vain deceit;
Their clothing is much like the saints,
But God abhors their false pretense.
Of God I feel constrained to go
And fill the station where I'm sent.
Farewell, dear friend, O think of me
When I am gone to come no more.

The Crisis and its Consequences.

We are in the revolutionary times. Blood has already been shed in the streets of Philadelphia, growing out of the conflict between the African and Anglo-Saxon races on this continent; and God only knows when the streets of all our other cities, from the Potomac to the borders of Canada, will be crimsoned from the same cause. It is about twenty years since the agitation and conflict between those races commenced in the city of Boston, and it has now reached a point that affects our churches, our parties, our politicians, our statesmen, and the great and vital interests of the republic. The whole country-- North and South, East and West--is now about to enter upon a re-agitation of this subject--an agitation of a most fearful revolutionary and bloodthirsty character, in reference to the African race of the South, and the Anglo Saxons of the whole Union. Previous to the meeting of the last Congress, the agitation of this sentiment was felt to such an extent as to harass political circles at Washington, and throughout the country, as the events, which subsequently transpired in that city fully, justify. In the lamentable condition of things which ensued, and the danger in which the Union was placed, the great patriots and statesmen of both parties--friends of the Union and of the constitution-- united their efforts in favor of conciliation, and went to work with the energy which characterized the revolutionary period of our history, and accomplished their patriotic purpose, by the passage of the bills known as the Compromise measures. But these very bills contain in them the germ of a new agitation, of a more horrible aspect and of a more bloody character than any that has taken place in this country within the last half century.

When the original Abolitionists commenced the agitation of the slavery question, twenty years ago, at the North, churches of every denomination were connected, and joined in the bonds of brotherhood--political parties were organized on general principles, and on a broad platform, throughout the United States--the democrats were united on certain general principles, and so were the whigs. In the course of time, however, and through the instrumentality of the Abolitionists, that agitation operated to such an extent as to break up the union, which previously existed between Northern and Southern churches, of every denomination except the Catholics. It has also broken up political parties, and severed the social and friendly ties, which existed between the Northern and Southern States. The same cause is, we fear, about to destroy the commercial relations, which exist between those sections of the republic; and the final consummation will, we fear, be the disruption of the Constitution and the Union, which have made this country what it is, and our people feared and respected throughout the whole civilized world. The compromise measures recently passed by both houses of Congress, have been seized upon by the Garrisons, Sewards, Weeds, Greeleys, and other Abolition fanatics of the North, and they are making them the subject of fresh agitation and excitement in New

England and in New York, and particularly on the Fugitive Slave bill. That measure is to form the principal plank of the new platform of the Abolitionists, of every character.

What is the fugitive slave law, and its character? Under the Constitution there can be no doubt of the perfect right of the masters of slaves to reclaim those who run away, and seek refuge in the Northern and non-slaveholding States. Objections have been made to the mode of recovery and reclamation provided in that bill, and a great deal of vituperation as been indulged in towards Congress, and towards the President, in consequence of the habeas corpus being suspended, and the fugitives being denied the right of a trial by jury. Let us examine this point a little. If, for instance, a person in New York is robbed of property to the amount of five hundred dollars, or any other sum, and the thief escapes to some Southern State, all we have to do is to send an officer after him, and bring him back to New York for trial and punishment. This is of common occurrence. Well, slaves, according to the laws of the Southern States as well as the Constitution of the United States, are property, and the fugitive slave bill operates precisely in the same way, by authorizing and demanding the reclamation of such property. If the Southern States choose to look upon slaves as property, it is a question with which the Northern States have nothing to do. At one time, we in New York, regarded them as property ourselves; and it was not until we found them unprofitable property, that we consented to the abolition of slavery.

Apart from the Fugitive Slave bill, the Southern people have, under the Constitution, a perfect right to demand reclamation of their fugitives; and yet, in the face of that contract between the States of this confederacy--in violation of that Constitution which was solemnly entered into by the thirteen original States, and which was signed by the immortal Washington and his compatriots, and which never would have been agreed to without the provision relative to Fugitive Slaves--we see the Abolitionists of the North, and a portion of the Whig party, opposing that law and that very provision of the Constitution, making their opposition to be the corner-stone of this new movement, and agitating the public mind to such an extent in connection with it, as perhaps to carry the next Congress under that rallying cry. The ultra-sentiments of Garrison and the original Abolitionists are precisely similar to those recently avowed by the Seward portion of the Whig party at their convention in Syracuse; so that, as far as the Slavery question is concerned, there is, to all intents and purposes, a union with them.

What, then, is the prospect before us? According to all appearances, the Slavery excitement is increasing every day, in every possible form and shape. Even some of the organs of the democratic party--the Evening Post in New York, and the Atlas in Albany--are favoring the destructive movement, and playing into the hands of the

Seward Abolitionists, and may possibly draw into their ranks Democratic Free Soilers enough to secure the success of the Syracuse ticket at the ensuing election. This renewed agitation is not confined to New York. Meetings are held in opposition to the Fugitive Slave bill in New England, also. The excitement is spreading and increasing, and out of the large cities there seems to be but one ground assumed on the question, and that is, opposition to the measures of compromise recently passed by Congress, without which this Union is not worth a straw, and would be shattered into a thousand fragments within five years. And according to all appearances, we would not be surprised to see the Seward abolition nominations put forward by the Syracuse convention, carried triumphantly at the next election, in consequence of the new Abolition effervescence, and the new movement undertaken by Seward and his associates, and this fresh outburst of anti-slavery sentiment. If such should be the case, and the next Congress should be elected under the cry of abolition, what would be the result? What is the prospect of a continuance of this Union for even two, three, or five years? The South is excited as much as the North, on this question, but in a different manner, and will not submit to the repeal of the Fugitive Slave bill, without one of the most terrible convulsions that has been witnessed in this country since the foundation of the government.

The prospect is indeed gloomy. The people of this city, and the friends of the Union, are sleeping on a mine of gunpowder that may explode at any moment, without the slightest warning. Apathy, inexcusable apathy, prevails amongst our merchants, our bankers, mechanics and businessmen of all kinds, whose interests depend upon the perpetuity of the Union. No one seems to perceive the importance of the terrible crisis, more terrible than any that we have yet experienced. We may as well prepare now, as at any time, and endeavor to ward off the dangers that assail us. If this abolition agitation go on, and the next elections shall be carried under the cry of abolition, we may make up our minds that a dissolution of the Union will take place in less than five years. This result is positive--certain--unchangeable as the laws of Nature. Look out for a social convulsion--prepare for revolution and blood.

From the *National Era.*

The Prospects of Slavery.

What will be the condition of the slave holding States at the end of the present century, should they maintain the system of slavery? In the year 1800, the free population of those States, counting New York, New Jersey, and Pennsylvania, as non-slaveholding, was 1,772,000; the slaves, 860,000. In 1850, the white population in the slave States is 6,410,000; the slaves, 3,075,000. We use round numbers. The increase of the free population during half a century has been at the rate of 260 per cent; of the slave, 243 per cent. Should the same ratio prevail for the next half century, the free population will amount to 23,072,000; the slave to, 10,513,000. This calculation assumes that all the States now holding slaves, will continue slaveholding till the year 1900; but this is not to be supposed. Already the free population is gaining rapidly on the slaves in Virginia, Maryland, Kentucky, Tennessee, and Missouri; while the reverse operation is going on in South Carolina, Georgia, Alabama, Mississippi, and Arkansas. The following table shows the tendency of things strikingly enough in Virginia:

1850.

- Whites . . . . . 894,000.
- Slaves . . . . . 475,972.
- Free-colored . . . . . 53,757.

1840.

- [Whites . . . . .] 791,000
- [Slaves . . . . .] 448,988
- [Free-colored . . . . .] 49,941

Increase.

- [Whites . . . . .] 103,000,
- [Slaves . . . . .] 26,984.
- [Free-colored . . . . .] 3,816.

In Maryland, the total population is as follows: 412,803 whites; 89,178 slaves; and 73,158 free negroes. The total increase in the State since 1840 is 107,573. The free negro population is now 73,1058, in 1840 it was 61,937, showing an increase of 11,221. The total slave population in 1840 was 89,719; it is now only 89,178! being an actual decrease of 541 in ten years!

On the other hand, in South Carolina and Mississippi the slaves have far outstripped the freemen. In the former in 1840 the free population was 266,305; in 1850, 283,737, showing an increase of 17,232; while in 1840 the slaves numbered 327,934, in 1850 384,720, showing an increase of 56,786. The ratio of increase for the free is but 6, 1 per cent; that for the slaves 17. 6 per cent. In Mississippi, the slaves numbered 20,000 more than the freemen. In Arkansas the ratio of slave increase for the last ten years has been 125 per cent; free, 83 per cent.

In view of these facts, it is not to be supposed that Maryland, Virginia, Kentucky, Tennessee, and Missouri will be slaveholding States much longer than twenty-five years to come; and it is probable that States which now contain one half the slave population will be free before the year 1900. The whole of the Slave population at that time, unless Slavery be sooner abolished, will be concentrated to the amount of ten or eleven millions within States which now contain a free population of only three millions; the increase of which is destined to proceed in a diminished ratio, while the ratio of the slave increase cannot be expected to fall off in any considerable degree. Indeed, we may fairly presume from the facts above stated, and from the tendency of slave labor to drive out the free laborer, that by the close of the present century, if Slavery continue, a slave population of ten millions will be collected within a section of country containing a numerically inferior free population.

Within the last century, slaves have steadily improved in intelligence. Have the causes of this improvement exhausted themselves, or are they not working with increased power and through additional channels?

The next fifty years will witness changes in their character which, considered in connection with their great numerical force, must awaken our gloomiest apprehensions, should the hand of power continue heavy upon them. But, should the South pass safely through the increasing perils of the next fifty years, can it then dream of the possibility of ten millions of men, who have had the benefit of white instruction and free example so many generations, submitting much longer to the domination of a less physical force than their own?

And what then will be the condition of the slaveholding section in other respects? Recollect, Virginia, Maryland, Kentucky, Missouri, will not be embraced within it. Cursed with a redundant slave population, its soil exhausted by thriftless culture, its staple rivaled in the markets of the world by a production now coming into notice, and which can be grown everywhere by free labor, with diminished returns from its crops, to be preyed upon by an increasing surplus of laborers, who must eat or be decimated, with no more slave territory to bring temporary reprieve, the slaveholders would be compelled to emancipate their slaves, or expatriate themselves. Let the alarmist paint the gloomiest pictures of the consequences of Emancipation his fancy can draw, a far deeper gloom hangs about the tremendous realities of the slavery that shall exist in the year 1900; if it be continued so long.

From the *New York Tribune.*

Michigan Politics--The State Election--Negro Suffrage, &c.

PAW PAW, Mich. Monday, Oct. 28.

Our general Election comes off the 5th of next month, and will be an important one. By an amendment in our Constitution, the following State officers are to be elected by the People (instead of being appointed, as before), viz: Secretary of State, Auditor General, State Treasurer, Attorney General, Superintendent of Public Instruction, and three Judges of the Supreme Court. We also elect Congressmen, State Legislature, and County officers generally. Among the latter a Prosecuting Attorney for each County, which office has been heretofore held by appointment. We are also to vote on the adoption of the new State Constitution, and on the question of extending the right of suffrage to the descendants of Africa. So you see we shall have voting enough, for once. What possible valid objection can be raised, in a country which recognizes the principle that 'the right to govern comes from the consent of the governed,' to allowing a man to vote because his skin happens to be a few shades darker and his hair to possess more and shorter kinks than another man's, is entirely beyond the comprehension of your correspondent. What man of common sense, who values his logical reputation is prepared to say that it would not be as just and reasonable to deny a man the common rights of citizenship because he may be red-haired, squint-eyed or wry-necked?--Yet much I fear that the people of this State will deny to the colored population the poor privilege of a voice in saying who shall tax, imprison or hang them--beg pardon, I was forgetting that we don't break necks judicially in this State now. I predict that the great mass of that party which labels itself 'Democratic'--which claims to be the exclusive friend of the poor man, the protector of the oppressed and lowly, and flaunts in every body's face, its banners inscribed with 'Equal Rights,' and all that sort of thing--will oppose this measure of justice. No, Sir, the patent Democracy of this State will not vote for universal suffrage. That party think 'niggers are very well in their place,' but it would be dangerous to trust them with the elective franchise, because they may not always vote the 'Democratic ticket.'

The Fugitive Slave Law is beginning to create some excitement, and will doubtless have some effect upon the Election, but the Locos will undoubtedly succeed in their State Ticket. We have nominated a strong Free Soil Whig (JOSEPH R. WILLIAMS) for Congress in this (2d) District. The opposition candidate is Hon. Charles E. Stewart, who was effectually and handsomely 'laid out' by Elder Sprague in 1848. I think that Williams will flog him as surely as did the Elder, but perhaps by a decreased majority.

In this County (Van Buren) the rival candidates for the Legislature are LYMAN A. FITCH, Whig, and MORGAN L. FITCH, Loco, brothers. As there is a Loco majority of about 100 in the County, it will be hard pulling for us; but, go as it will, "it's all in the family."

Yours,

WOLVERINE.

NARRATIVE CONTINUED.

CHAPTER VII.

In the latter part of the last Chapter of the first edition of my Narrative, I omitted a very interesting fact, in relation to my obtaining the evidence of my acceptance with the Savior.

On the Saturday (previous to the Monday spoken of), I left the city of Philadelphia, for the purpose of attending a Quarterly Meeting, some eighteen miles distance at a place called Dutch Town, in the State of New Jersey, under the supervision of the Rev. John Cornish, who was at that time Elder in charge of the New Jersey Circuit. My mind, as I have previously stated, was powerfully exercised. I felt that there was a work for me to do, and I went to the meeting, hoping that I might meet with an opportunity of saying something by way of exhortation, and to warn poor sinners to flee the wrath to come. I arrived there in the evening in time for meeting, which I attended. But there was no opportunity afforded me. I went home with a friend, with whom I spent the night. The next morning, being the Sabbath, I was taken with a very strange feeling--my mind became filled with doubts and despair. A state of tremor and horror seized my frame, and the heavens seemed as brass to me. I felt as though I was undone for ever, and that God was angry with me. I spent the day in deep distress of mind, walking with my arms folded, for it seemed that I could find no rest or ease. I tried to pray, but it seemed that my prayers went no higher than my head. I at one time thought that I would be damned before the sun set, and when setting, it looked to me like a ball of fire. The following day, Monday, I started for home where I arrived late in the afternoon. I was at that time boarding in the family of my father-in-law, Leander Lee, who resided in Prune-street, near Fourth. By this time, I felt somewhat relieved from my former state of feelings, and felt as though I should like to attend a religious meeting. Accordingly, I started for Class, and on the way called to see a family by the name of BLACK, in Elizabeth-street, where I had previously kept house. While there, I was talking with the old lady and her daughter Hatty, on the subject of religion.

They exhorted me to believe on the Lord Jesus Christ, as did Paul, the jailer. Acts xvi. 31, and all at once faith sprang up and laid hold on the rich promises of the Saviour, and as quick as thought I felt the change, and was enabled to cry out in the language of the Psalmist, David, "The Lord is my Shepherd, I shall not want. He maketh me to lie down in green pastures; he leadeth me beside the still waters." That was the happiest hour that I had ever experienced in all the days of my life. I resided in the city of Philadelphia some fifteen years--during that time, I continued my membership in the A. M. E. Bethel Church, which is located on the corner of Sixth and Lombard streets. During my residence there, I followed various kinds of employment, such as keeping a Clothingcellar, Waiting, and public Portering, attending Store, &c. During that time I married again, and soon became surrounded with domestic cares, which gave me the impulse of mind that it was a duty enjoined upon me to engage in procuring property for the comfort of myself and family. Accordingly I purchased in 1834, a small estate in the city of Camden, New Jersey, where I resided for

a few months. In the autumn of the same year, I removed back to the city of Philadelphia. Having for a long time felt it to be my duty to travel, and labor for the good of souls, I accordingly in the Spring of 1836, made application for Preacher's License, which I received from the hands of the Rt. Rev. Bishop Brown, who was at that time preacher in charge of the said A. M. E. Bethel Church.

CHAPTER VIII.

My appointment to the Jersey Circuit under the Supervision
of the Rev. Wm. Moore.

Early in the month of July, 1836, I entered upon the discharge of my duties as a subordinate, where I traveled the remainder of the year. While upon that Circuit, we experienced a degree of suffering. The Circuit was quite extensive, and the people generally poor, and unable in very many instances to afford us a comfortable living. We found it extremely unpleasant in the winter season, the traveling being bad, &c.; yet, in the midst of this, myself and senior had the pleasure of seeing the work of the Lord prospering in our hands, and many souls I trust were happily converted to God.

There were some incidents which occurred during the year, which were somewhat trying in their nature. The state of New Jersey was much infested with "Kidnappers," who were prowling about in several of the communities through which we had to pass. On one occasion they made an arrest of a young colored man at a place called Sand-town. The nature of the case is as follows: they secured the services of a white man, (who must have been of a nefarious character, and lived in the vicinity, where this colored man's family resided,) who went in company with the band of man-stealers, and at a late hour of the night, rapped at the door of this colored family's house, when the lady from within asked who was there? the reply was 'a friend.' He continued by asking, 'is your husband at home?' when she (the lady) wished to know what he wanted with him; his reply was, to see him about going to work to-morrow. He asked the lady if she would not rise and let him in, as he was cold and wanted to warm himself. Supposing him to be a neighbor, after hesitating a while, she arose and opened the door, when he entered, and made his way to the fire-place with a candle in hand. The fire being covered over for the night, he stuck the candle in the embers and lighted it. This was no sooner done than the whole gang rushed in. This young man, before mentioned, in company with two others, were upstairs in bed, when upon hearing what was going on below, supposing that all was not right, prepared themselves to make battle; but two of them becoming frightened, jumped out from a window and made their escape. The other seized a loaded gun, that was in their room, and aimed at his antagonist, but for the want of moral courage, he failed in the attempt, when his adversary seized him and carried him off in fetters, to a place called Sweetsborough, some eight or ten miles distant; where they placed him in the garret of a tavern to await the arrival of others, whom they designed to capture. This was on a Friday evening. There was a settlement of colored people at a place called Dutchtown, some half mile distance, who on hearing of the circumstances, were determined to go to the rescue of their fellow man. Accordingly, on the following Sabbath, at night after maturing their plans they went to the scene of action, and surrounded the tavern. The captivators were all drinking, carousing and sporting over their victim, when the colored people without were armed with guns, pistols, and missiles of various kinds, let go a volley of stone shots, &c. through the doors and windows; the lights within were immediately blown out, and shots were fired from within. There was a pedlar who had put up there for the night, and upon hearing the rupture below which broke upon his nightly vision, and starting from his slumber, in passing down stairs, they, supposing him to be their captive, one of the party immediately shot him, but fortunately the wound was not mortal.

This as a matter of course created a great excitement, nevertheless, all was kept perfectly quiet until the following Tuesday, when they had mustered up their volunteers, and started for the colored settlement, to route and capture their opposing party. Their presence in the settlement was like the "Black plague" in Europe, or the seven headed hydra. Men, women and children, absconding and leaving their domiciles unoccupied, fleeing before their pursuers in various directions. Upon the night of the outbreak I was at an appointment at a place called Hagerstown, near Salem, a distance of some ten or fifteen miles. My colleague, Rev. W. Moore, was in the settlement at the time the occurrence took place. He had for some days previous complained of not being well, and was on his way returning to Philadelphia.

I was upon my upward tour, and had to pass through Sweedsborough to get to my next appointment, where I arrived about eleven or twelve o'clock in the day, and as I drew near the tavern, I cast my eye that way and saw the broken doors and windows, and the bottles of King Alcohol exposed to public view; at that moment I heard them laughing and talking in a jolly manner, but as soon as they saw me I heard them say "there goes a nigger now." Just at that moment, I saw a tavern loafer come out and started off on a run towards the village, as this tavern stood upon the outskirts of the town. On seeing this, my mind became somewhat alarmed, believing that his designs were to do me an injury, and accordingly upon my arrival in the village I discovered a large crowd rushing from another tavern with guns, pistols, bludgeons, hounds, &c. I supposed the infuriated mob intended to rush upon me; but instead of doing so, it seems to me that fear suddenly came upon them, which appeared to quell their maddened rage. God be praised for this deliverance, for our enemies, we see them to-day, and to-morrow they are no more. In passing on I had a small bridge to cross beyond the end of which the roads forked. I met two or three gangs returning from their exploring expeditions, and as they met, I heard one party say to the other, "we have got Murray the Class Leader." They had already captured several whom they had incarcerated in Woodbury jail. When I arrived at the settlement, there was not a vestige to be seen.--The place looked forlorn, the houses that had but a few days before been occupied by their inmates, were now forsaken and looked desolate. After viewing this state of things I left for the upper part of the Circuit where I remained until such time that things became quiet in that vicinity. There were several arrests made during the year in various portions of the State, some of which were of a very serious nature; the brother and his wife, at whose house I frequently staid when at my appointment in that place, were very kind and hospitable. Soon after I left the Circuit, he was decoyed by a nefarious white man, who lived neighbor to him. The scheme of operation was as follows: The white man pretended that he had lost some of his cattle, and wished to secure his services in hunting them; this was early in the morning, as he was weeding his garden, his wife at this time was preparing breakfast within doors. He not having the slightest suspicion of any thing wrong, promised to comply with his wishes in securing his cattle. Accordingly after breakfast he started off with his supposed friend--they had not proceeded far before he was delivered into the hands of his captivators, who were concealed in the woods some three hundred yards from the house. Oh! the blighting and withering curse of American Slavery which regards not the situations, circumstances or condition of the poor colored people or the descendants of Africa, but spreads devastation and destruction more or less throughout the American continent.

Having travelled the year out under adverse circumstances in the spring of 1837, I met the Annual

Conference in the city of Philadelphia, as I was a candidate upon trial for the Itinerant service, according to the usage of the A. M. E. Church. During the year, I became much reduced in pecuniary circumstances. My little property that I had purchased previous to my going upon the Circuit, was neither finished or paid for. In view of the above, I deemed it proper and expedient to resume a located capacity until such times as I could redeem myself from the many responsibilities resting upon me.

CHAPTER IX.

The last seven years of my residence in Philadelphia.

Late in the summer of 1837, I engaged in the beer business; finding it to be a lucrative pursuit, I made it a business during the spring and summer seasons, and in the winter I followed teaming, together with other pursuits, and it was not long before I had accumulated a considerable stock in the way of horses, wagons, carts, &c., and was compelled to keep several hands in my employ. During the seven years, I was enabled to redeem myself from many of my personal responsibilities, also to realize a comfortable living, and to procure some additional property, but not without much perseverance and industry, working late and early; being surrounded with peculiar circumstances, I had my troubles in common as other men, and yet during that time I often felt that God had a more noble work for me, and that a city business life was not the sphere of action for me. Accordingly, in the autumn of 1844, I wound up my business at a sacrifice, and on the 28th day of October, I left the busy scenes of a crowded metropolis and started for New York.

Nothing worthy of note occurred on my passage. I arrived at New York in the Empire City, where I spent some two or three days in visiting my friends, during which time I associated myself with the Rev. E. N. Hall, who at that time had the supervision of the A. M. E.

Church, in High street, Brooklyn, Long Island. Late on a Saturday afternoon, I took my leave of him and started on my mission, taking the cars at South ferry, and proceeded down the Island, and soon found myself among strangers. The night fall was fast approaching, when my mind began to feel sad, not knowing where I should find a friend or a home for the night. However after arriving at a place called "Farmingdale" some thirty miles distant, down on the island; I there left the cars and went on foot in pursuit of a home for the night when I fell in company with a man, who, in the course of conversation, directed me to a colored gentleman by the name of Thompson; after wandering in the night some one or two miles, I found the house standing in a lonely country place. Upon rapping at the door, I found that the good man and his family had retired to bed. He arose and invited me in. I informed him that I was a stranger, and my errand was that of a Missionary; that I had been recommended to him by a gentleman, who thought that I would be likely to be accommodated for that night. I found him and his lady to be very fine people. The next morning being the Sabbath they invited me to accompany them to church, a distance of some three miles, to a place called Huntingdon, which invitation I readily accepted. Upon our arrival at church, I soon found myself in the midst of the people of God, who very kindly invited me to preach for them, which I tried to do, and it pleased the Lord to make bare his arm in the midst of the congregation. Just before entering the pulpit, I discovered a very ancient, venerable looking gentleman.

He looked as though he might be of the "Indian origin."
His locks were much silvered, his head bespoke the frost
of many winters, by reason of age he was quite bowed
down towards the earth. I discovered that he paid much
attention to the discourse, and seemed to get quite happy,
so much, so that before the meeting closed, he arose and
said that he had not been to meeting for a long time by
reason of age and infirmity. But said he the Lord told me
that a stranger was to preach here this morning, and I was
bound to find my way to this place. At the close of the
services the congregation dispersed, and went to their
respective homes, and in the evening they came up for
worship, and I was invited to address them again. I
endeavored to do so, and in the course of my remarks I
stated that there was someone present or in that
neighborhood who would die before three weeks.
Accordingly, it was so. This remark was regarded by
many, and has often been the subject of conversation
since, as I have been informed. On the following
Tuesday, I left there for a place called "Setaucket," where
I stopped with a family by the name of Tobias. I found his
lady to be an excellent woman, with them I spent several
days. While there I was informed that their house was
once the scene of fiddling and dancing, until a very
serious circumstance occurred, which was as follows:--
On one occasion they had fiddling and dancing, when one
of the party who had over exerted himself upon the floor,
retired to one side of the room, and seated himself upon a
chair. While the merry crowd were amusing themselves,

one of the guests stepped up and invited him to take another seat--but lo! the man was dead!--from the ball-room, he went to the Judgment seat of Christ. While in that vicinity, I visited and preached in several places, to both white and colored, viz: Port Jefferson, Stony Brook, Drowned Meadows, so called from the inundation of the freshet, which overflowed the flats, Mount Misery, which name took its origin from a poor sailor, who was cast away in a great storm, while his comrades all perished. He was washed upon the shore; while there his dying groans brought to his rescue some one, who by chance passed that way. Also at a place called Old Man; from there I went to Riverhead, where I preached to a white congregation, from these words, "And Moses said unto Hobab, the son of Raguel, the Midianite, Moses' father-in-law, We are journeying unto the place of which the Lord said, I will give it you: come thou with us, and we will do thee good: for the Lord hath spoken good, concerning Israel."--Numbers x. 29. There was an elderly gentleman quite corpulent, who seemed much pleased with the discourse, and said he had been upon his journey a long while. The next place I visited was called Flanders, where I held meeting in a country schoolhouse. While addressing the congregation, I was interrupted by a lowbred person, who was a pest to the community. On the following morning I left for a place called Good-ground, where I arrived about noon, and called upon a gentleman by the name of Allmon Squires, with whom I took dinner. Himself and lady were very kind, and urged me to spend the night with them, but hearing of an Indian settlement some mile and a half distant, I preferred going there for the night. On my way thither, in passing through a skirt of woods, I saw from the roadside, two graves, one enclosed while the other lay without, side by side; the one enclosed had a large marble tombstone at the head, with this inscription upon it. "Here lies the remains of the Rev. Paul Cuffee, who was educated by the New York Missionary Society and was sent as a missionary to civilize this illmannered people called the Chinecock tribe." This tribe owns some five hundred acres of land and have their own internal laws inherent from their ancestors. The following is one of their laws in relation to marriage:

No person is allowed to settle among them unless one of the party, he or she, be wedded to a member of the tribe. In that case they are allowed to settle. They follow for a livelihood, fishing, gunning, &c. The country abounds with wild fowl. They seem to have no disposition to cultivate the soil; hence they derive little or nothing but what grows spontaneously. The tribe is quite civilized, and are very friendly and hospitable. They had a missionary among them at that time, by the name of Priest Benjamin. Among this friendly people I stayed some one or two weeks, during which time I held several religious meetings with them, and on the Sabbath I was to take my leave from them. I preached for them in the morning, during which there was scarcely a dry eye in the whole congregation. Since then I was informed it produced abundant good. In the afternoon, I left for a place called Southampton, where I preached to a white Methodist congregation. The next day, Monday, I left for "Sag Harbor." There I found a colored church and congregation (who were of the Zion connection,) for whom I preached several times, and then left for Greenport, which is the extreme end of Long Island, some ninety-five miles distant from the city of New York. Greenport is located at the head of navigable waters where there is every facility for the travelling public, between Boston and New York. The town was in quite a flourishing condition, and bid fair to monopolize, and do a considerable business. While at this place I stopped with a family named Boothe. I found himself and lady to be very fine people. They lived very comfortably, and had by their industry accumulated quite a handsome little property.

CHAPTER X.

My Tour in the State of Connecticut.

I arrived in New London Ct. on Christmas day, 1844. This I found to be quite a large and flourishing town, located on the Quinebaug river, with some five or six thousand inhabitants who were chiefly engaged in farming and mechanical pursuits, and to some extent in the Whale Fishery. While there, I stopped with a colored family by the name of Anderson. There are quite a number of colored people in that place who are living without any regular established organized system of religion among themselves. During my stay I held meetings for them several times, and then left for the city of Norwich, Ct. Here I found a still larger number of colored people, who were more desirous of improvement in social, moral and religious habits, for the accomplishment of which they had associated themselves in times past, and built for themselves a meeting house, but being of different opinions in relation to the mode of religious worship dissensions, and divisions had crept in their midst, which finally resulted in serious altercations, so much so that the house was closed, and seldom ever opened for religious meetings except when a stranger would pass along. On the eve of my departure from them they urged me to visit them again, which I promised to do within three weeks, but was unable to do so, being more successful in other places. From there I went to Stonington, Ct. This is a town on the South-east coast on the L. I. Sound. Its commercial interest is principally dependant upon the whale fishery, and its location also affords very favorable facilities for the transportation of merchandise and the traveling public. The colored people of this place, number between one and two hundred, and there having been no religious organization among them, for their social and moral elevation, I called a meeting, and at the close of which I made known to them my mission. They at once entered into the spirit of having a religious organization for their present and future happiness upon the promise that I would return in the course of a few days. I left for lands that I had not yet seen, and went to Providence, R. I. This I found to be a large and flourishing city, with some thirty or forty thousand inhabitants. Its location is on Naraganset Bay, and the inhabitants are chiefly employed in manufacturing pursuits. Here I spent several days, forming acquaintances with friends whom I had not heretofore seen. I found the colored people possessing much intelligence and very enterprising. There are very many of them who by their industry have amassed a considerable amount of property.

Here I found the Rev. Jacob Matthews who had the supervision of the A. M. E. Society for whom I preached once or twice. While there I stopped with a family by the name of Henson. I found this to be an excellent family. I also formed a slight acquaintance with several other respectable families. This ending my visit I left on a Saturday afternoon for the purpose of returning to Stonington.

I went to the depot. The cars started and I supposed they were gone. I ran the length of the platform for the purpose of jumping on board, reaching the end before I was aware. I fell with my head within a few inches of the rail, over which forty cars were then passing and the bystanding crowd supposing that I was killed, rushed to see. Having the presence of mind (as I fell) I rolled from the track. Thus by the mercy of God I escaped premature death. After recovering a little from my fright, I soon learned that the cars were not gone, but were running up for the purpose of hitching to other cars. I seated myself in the cars, and soon arrived at Stonington, where I spent the Sabbath; and in the evening I formed a Society of some sixteen members, unto whom I preached occasionally through the winter, during which time the Society increased to some thirty members. While absent from Stonington, I visited a place called "Charlestown" (an Indian settlement of the Naraganset tribe,) in the state of Rhode Island. This tribe is quite civilized, and more in habituated to agricultural pursuits, and were very friendly and hospitable. They were engaged in holding a series of religious meetings, which I found productive of a good state of feeling in their midst with several conversions. During my stay, I attended many of their meetings and visited them in their families. I also was induced to visit their place of burial, which was in the woods, and was not a little amused while walking among the graves of their dead in noticing their form of burial. Their graves were covered with brush, rubbish &c. Their tombstones were rough flagg. Beneath them lay the chieftain and the man of war. During my stay I received an invitation to preach at a country farm house some three miles distant. The night was extremely cold, being in the middle of winter. The earth was clad in its white garment of snow, upon which the hoary frost was fast falling; while the moon shone with magnificent splendor and sparkling upon the bosom of the snow like the twinkling stars that guide the wayward traveller upon his exploring expeditions in distributing benevolence to his fellow-men.

From this place, I returned to Stonington to visit the infant Society that I had previously formed. After spending a day or two there I took a tour to Boston, Massachusetts, where I spent a few days with kind friends. I stopped with the family of the Rev. H. J. Johnson. While there I was taken sick, and received the kindest treatment from himself and lady. On recovering, I left Boston, for Worcester, Ms. Here I found the character of the colored people much degraded with some few exceptions. I arrived in Worcester on a Friday evening, and stopped with a family by the name of Hemanway, and while there they gave me a full statement of the colored people of that place, which was truly humiliating. However, I was anxious to get a meeting among them. Accordingly, on a Saturday morning I started out for the purpose of giving notice that I would preach for them on the Sabbath, providing they would furnish a place. In order to become satisfied with their condition, I went from house to house, and gave notice to some ten or fifteen families, that I would hold a religious meeting for them on the following day (Sunday.)

Finally, it was agreed upon that the meeting should be held at the school house, that was occupied by a colored school. An individual was sent to the schoolmistress, to enquire whether the house could be secured. She informed the person that it could be secured, and afterward took the key and placed it in the hands of the school committee. Hence we were disappointed in obtaining the house; the meeting was therefore held at the house of Mrs. Banselea, where we had some half dozen in attendance, one of whom had been very active in hunting for a place, and I was going to say, that he was so drunk that he could not sit upon a chair, without falling. With this state of things I became disgusted, and dispatched a man with a note to the pastor of the Methodist Church to know of him, if I could have the use of his Rostrum, for the purpose of holding a religious meeting. Upon his return, after being some time absent, I asked him if he saw the clergyman, to which he replied "he did" and that I must go with him and see the gentleman; at this suggestion, I started off in company with him. But not feeling in my own mind, that all things were right, I asked him if he had seen the clergyman, and what he said. "He said no, but I guess he wants to see you."

At this moment, I felt tried in my mind, and told him to take the note and see that the gentleman read it, and bring me a correct answer. With this he started off and did not return until late in the afternoon, when he stated that I was to meet the gentleman at the vestry of his church about six o'clock in the evening. Accordingly I met him there and he asked what I wished. I asked him if he had not received a note from me that afternoon and if the note did not state my wishes. At this he hemmed and hossed, and said that he did not understand it. I then told him that I was a stranger, and my errand was that of a missionary, and I wished to secure his vestry, for the purpose of holding a religious meeting. He asked me when. I stated whenever it would meet his convenience, when it was finally agreed that I should have it upon the following evening (Monday,) and stated he would give notice to his congregation, but he would not be present. Accordingly on Monday evening I went to the vestry, where I found a group of despicable colored people. Upon my entering the pulpit they burst out into a roar of contemptible laughter. After concluding the opening hymn, I went to prayers, and asked God to have mercy upon, and save those poor miserable wretched beings. Upon rising from my knees, and looking over the room, I suppose that there were about a dozen persons altogether, both white and colored, and in that number there was but two respectable looking ones in the company, and they were white ladies, and looked as though they might be members of said church. I stated that I did not think that there would be any congregation there that night, and therefore I should decline preaching and took up my hat and left. The next day I left, and returned to Stonington, where I spent some time in regulating the Society. And on the first day of March, 1845, I started for Philadelphia where I spent a few weeks with an intention to return, after securing competent credentials from under the hands of Rev. Bishop Brown. While I was at Philadelphia an individual by the name of T. James, hearing of the Society at Stonington, and of my absence he went there and succeeded in scattering the people. I received a letter to that effect, and upon my return, I found that he had got one half of the people disaffected, so much so that the entire prospect was blasted. After remaining there a few days, I left, and again visited Providence, R. I, and from there to Boston, Mass. and then returned to Norwich, Conn. I remained there until the annual conference in New York city, where I met and joined the Itinerancy and was sent to Norwich. During that year I purchased a lot of ground and built a church, getting quite a large congregation and established a Sabbath school, all of which was in a flourishing condition when I left at the end of the year for conference. The following year, 1846, I was sent to the city of Providence, R. I., where I staid two years, during which time I found that the Society had been established some nine years, and were still worshipping in a school house that had been built by a company to whom it

belonged. Finding this to be the condition of the people, I went to work and persuade them to buy the house, which they did. We then went to work and remodeled and enlarged, and when finished, they found themselves in possession of a handsome property.

During my two years in Providence, I found the citizens, both white and colored, a very kind and interesting set of people.

I close by saying that I have been prompted by the purest motives to write this brief Narrative. I have written, hoping it may be a benefit to some in whose hands it may perchance to fall. God's name be glorified, and the author saved in the covenant of His grace.

CHRISTMAS ADDRESS,

Delivered before the Congregation of the First Colored American
Congregational Methodist Church, by the Pastor, Rev. L. TILMON, Dec. 25, 1853.

DEAR BRETHREN AND SISTERS,

By the mercy of God, many of us have been spared to see another Christmas. While many since the last, with whom we have often associated, are no more--they have gone the way of all the earth. During the past, we have experienced troubles too numerous to mention; in the midst of which, we have been compelled to break off our social relation from the mother church. In consequence of which, many unpleasant things have been said about us, which we have had to endure. Though we have been persecuted, we have not been destroyed--cast down but not forsaken--but we have been preserved in the hour of temptation. Many with whom we have associated in times past, and have walked together to the house of God, have also become our enemies, for some trivial cause or other. These things ought not so to be, for they strew our pathway with sorrows to the grave: while our pleasures are mingled with grief. All this ariseth upon the ground of our cherishing those dissentions as did ancient Israel in the wilderness, which greatly retarded their onward progress to the land of their heavenly Canaan. This has been our situation during the past year. In the mean time when present, I have visited many of your families and with you have mingled in the social family circle.

And I have stood by the bed side of your sick and dying--I have christened your children--I have attended the funerals of your dead--I have walked with you to the field of graves--I have married your sons and your daughters. We are now upon the eve of another year; and in view of the past, we should let a different course of conduct mark the future. For we too, like our friends and acquaintances are passing away, and perhaps this may be our last. Time will blot out our existence, and we shall be as though we never were. We should therefore labor to cherish the highest regard one for the other. The peculiar circumstances with which we are surrounded, as a church demands our most serious attention for its future prosperity. The enemy of all righteousness is upon the alert, therefore we need a great deal of patience. As the Apostle says "Brethren ye have need of patience; after ye have done the will of God, that ye might receive the promise," for these are the days that tries men's souls. Disappointments and diseases walk abroad in the land, and in common with our fellow men we may expect to share a portion. In our midst are the aged poor, and the lonely widow--they too demand our care and regard; for the Scripture tells us, "He that giveth to the poor lendeth to the Lord." There are also attached to our congregation many young people, who need much instruction, both by way of precept and example, to aid them on in the path of life, and to induce others to seek an interest in the Savior.

And there too is the Sabbath School room, which is considered by some to be the minor department of the church, upon which we cannot place too high a regard, for it is the nursery, from which the church among other sources must be perpetuated. This department affords a field sufficiently large in which all may find room to labor. This department also imposes a duty upon parents, fathers, mothers, brothers and sisters. To train up their children in their social family circles around the hearth stone. Brethren and Sisters, the above are some of the most serious duties that demand our attention. We must therefore look to the future as well as the present, for both civil, political and religious institutions, have all had their rise and fall, and during their state of prosperity, they have had to contend with all that were opposed to their rise and elevation. And we too, may expect to share the same like afflictions, for we have not yet reached the place of our destination, but are in the wilderness.

> When I can read my title clear
> To mansions in the skies,
> I'll bid farewell to every fear,
> And wipe my weeping eyes.
> There is a rest remaining for
> The people of God.

THE DESTINY OF MAN.

Man is formed for action, as well as for contemplation. For this purpose, there are interwoven in his constitution, powers, principles, instincts, feelings, and affections, which have a reference to his improvement in virtue, and which excite him to promote the happiness of others--these powers and active principles like the intellectual, are susceptible of vast improvement, by attention, exercise, trials and difficulties, and by an expansion of the intellectual views. Such are filial and fraternal affection, fortitude, temperance, justice, gratitude, generosity, love of friends and country, philanthropy and general benevolence. Degenerate as our world has always been, many striking examples of such virtues have been displayed both in ancient and modern times, which demonstrate the vigor, expansion and sublimity of the moral powers of man.

When we behold men animated by noble sentiments, exhibiting sublime virtues and performing illustrious actions--displaying generosity and beneficence in seasons of calamity and tranquility, and fortitude in the midst of difficulties and dangers--desiring riches only for the sake of distributing them--estimating places of power and honor, only for the sake of suppressing vice, rewarding virtue, and promoting the prosperity of their country-- suffering injuries and affronts with patience and serenity-- stifling resentment when they have it in their power to inflict vengeance-- displaying kindness and generosity towards enemies and slanderers--vanquishing irascible passions and licentious desires in the midst of the strongest temptations--submitting to pain and disgrace in order to promote the prosperity of friends and relatives--and sacrificing repose, honors, wealth, and even life itself, for the good of their country or for promoting the best interests of the human race, we perceive in such examples features of the human mind which mark its dignity and grandeur, and indeed its destination to a higher scene of action and enjoyment.

Even in the annals of the pagan world, we find many examples of such illustrious virtues--there we read of Regulus exposing himself to the most cruel torments and to death itself, rather than suffer his veracity to be called in question--Of Phocion, who exposed himself to the fury of an enraged assembly, by inveighing against the vices, and endeavoring to promote the best interests of his countrymen--and gave it as his last command to his son, when he was going to execution, "that he should forget how ill the Athenians had treated his father"--Of Cyrus, who was possessed of wisdom, moderation, courage, magnanimity and noble sentiments, and who employed them all to promote the happiness of his people--Of Scipio, in whose actions the virtues of generosity and liberality, goodness, gentleness, justice, magnanimity and chastity shone with distinguished luster--and of Damon and Pythias, who were knit together in the bonds of friendship, which all the terrors of an ignominious death could not dissolve. But of all the characters of the heathen world, illustrious for virtue, Aristides appears to stand in the foremost rank, an extraordinary greatness of soul, (says Rollin) made him superior to every passion, interest, pleasure, ambition, resentment, jealousy, were extinguished in him by the love of virtue and his country. The merit of others, instead of offending him, became his own by the approbation he gave it. He rendered the government of the Athenians amiable to their allies, by his mildness, goodness, humanity and justice. The disinterestedness he showed in the management of the public treasure, and the love of poverty which he carried almost to an excess, are virtues so far superior to the practice of our age, that they scarce seem credible to us. His conduct and principles were always uniform, steadfast in the pursuit of whatever he thought just--and incapable of the least falsehood or shadow of flattery, disguise, or fraud, even in jest. He had such a control over his passions that he uniformly sacrificed his private interests and his private resentments to the good of the public.

Themistocles was one of the principal actors who procured his banishment from Athens, but after being recalled, he assisted him on every occasion with his advice and credit joyfully, taking pains to promote the glory of his enemy through the motive of advancing the public good, and when afterwards the disgrace of Themistocles gave him a proper opportunity for revenge, instead of resenting the ill treatment he had received from him, he constantly refused to join with his enemies, being as far from secretly rejoicing over the misfortune of his adversary as he had been before from being afflicted at his good success. Such virtues reflect a dignity and grandeur on every mind in which they reside, which appear incompatible with the idea that it is destined to retire forever from the scene of action at the hour of death.

But the noblest examples of exalted virtue, are to be found among those who have enlisted themselves in the cause of Christianity. The Apostle Paul was an illustrious example of everything that is noble, heroic, generous and benevolent in human conduct. His soul was inspired with a holy ardor in promoting the best interest of mankind. To accomplish this object, he parted with his friends and relatives--relinquished his native country and everything that was dear to himself either as a Jew or as a Roman citizen, and exposed himself to persecution and dangers of every description.

During the prosecution of his benevolent career, he was "in journeying, often in perils of waters; in perils of robbers; in perils by his own countrymen, in perils by the heathen; in perils in the city; in perils in the wilderness; in perils in the sea; in perils among false brethren; in weariness and painfulness, in watchings, often in hunger and thirst, in fasting, often in stripes above measure, in cold and nakedness,"-- yet none of these things moved him, nor did he count his life dear to him, provided he might finish his course with joy, and be instrumental in accomplishing the present and eternal happiness of his fellow-men. In every period of the Christian era, similar characters have arisen to demonstrate the power of virtue and to bless mankind. Our own age and country have produced numerous philanthropic characters, who have shone as lights in the moral world, and have acted as benefactors to the human race. The names of Alfred, Penn, Barnard, Raikes, Neilde, Clarkson, Sharpe, Buxton, Wilberforce, Venning, and many others, are familiar to every one who is in the least acquainted with the annals of benevolence. The exertions which some of these individuals have made in the cause of liberty--in promoting the education of the young, in alleviating the distresses of the poor, in meliorating the condition of the prisoner, and in counteracting the abominable traffic in Slaves, will be felt as blessings conferred on mankind throughout succeeding generations, and will doubtless be held in everlasting remembrance.

But among all the philanthropic characters of the past or present age, the labors of the late Mr. Howard, stand pre-eminent. This illustrious man, from a principle of pure benevolence, devoted the greater part of his life to active beneficence, and to the alleviation of human wretchedness in every country where he travelled-- diving into the depth of dungeons, and exposing himself to the infected atmosphere of hospitals and jails, in order to meliorate the condition of the unfortunate, and to allay the sufferings of the mournful prisoner. In prosecuting the labors of love, he travelled three times through France,

four times through Italy, once through Spain and
Portugal, and also through Denmark, Sweden, Russia,
Poland and part of the Turkish empire, surveying the
haunts of misery, and distributing benefits to mankind
wherever he appeared.

From realm to realm with cross or crescent crowned,
O'er burning sands, deep waves, or wilds of snow,
Mild Howard journeying, seeks for haunts of woe
Down many a winding step to dungeon dark--
Where anguish wails aloud and fetters clank.
To caves bestrewed with many a mouldering bone,
And cells whose echoes only learn to groan;
Where no kind ears a whispering friend disclose--
No sun-beam enters, and no zephyr blows.
He treads, unconscious of fame or wealth,
Profuse of toil and prodigal of health;
Leads stern-ey'd justice to the dark domains,
If not to sever, to relax the chains.

Gives to her babes the self-devoted wife
To her fond husband liberty and life.
Onward he goes; disease and death retire
And murmuring demons hate and admire.

DARIUS.

The African Chief, Brogart.

"Chained in the market place he stood
A man of giant frame
Amid the gathering multitude
That shrunk to hear his name.
All stern of look and strong of limb,
His dark eye on the ground,
And silently they gazed on him
As on a lion bound.

Vainly, but well that chief had fought,
He was a captive now,
Yet pride that fortune humbles not
Was written on his brow.
The scars his dark, broad bosom wore
Showed warrior true and brave,
A prince among his tribe before;
He could not be a slave.

Then to his conqueror he spake,
"My brother is a king;
Undo this necklace from my neck,
And take this bracelet ring,
And send them where my brother reigns,
And I will fill thy hand

With stores of ivory from the land"
And gold dust from the sands."

Not for thy ivory nor thy gold
Will I unbind thy chain;
That bloody hand shall never hold
The battle spear again.
A price thy nation never gave
Shall yet be paid for thee,
For thou shalt be the Christian's slave
In lands beyond the sea,

Then wept the warrior chief and bade
To shred his locks away;
And one by one each heavy braid
Before the victor lay.
Thick were the plaited locks, and long
And deeply hidden there,
Shone many a ridge of gold, among
The dark and crispen hair.

Look, feast thy greedy eye with gold,
Long kept for direst need;
Take it--(thou askest sums untold)--
And say that I am freed.
Take it--my wife, the long long day
Weeps by the cocoa tree,

And my young children leave their play,
And ask in vain for me.

I take thy gold--but I have made
Thy fetters fast and strong,
And mean that by the cocoa shade
Thy wife shall wait thee long.
Strong was the agony that shook
The captive's frame to hear,
And the proud meaning of his look
Was changed to mortal fear.

His heart was broken, crazed his brain,
At once his eye grew wild.
He struggled fiercely with his chain,
Whispered, and wept and smiled;
Yet wore not long those fatal bands
For once, at shut of day,
The drew him forth upon the sands
The foul hyena's prey."

www.ingramcontent.com/pod-product-compliance
Lightning Source LLC
LaVergne TN
LVHW081324060426
835511LV00011B/1833